T4-ADM-970

NEW ZEALAND'S UNIQUE BIRDS

NEW ZEALAND'S
Unique Birds

BRIAN GILL *Curator of Birds, Auckland Museum*
PHOTOGRAPHS BY GEOFF MOON O.B.E.

REED

Published by Reed Books, a division of Reed Publishing (NZ) Ltd, 39 Rawene Rd, Birkenhead, Auckland.
Associated companies, branches and representatives throughout the world.
Website: www.reed.co.nz

This book is copyright. Except for the purpose of fair reviewing, no part of this publication may be reproduced or transmitted in any form or by any means, electronic or mechanical, including photocopying, recording, or any information storage and retrieval system, without permission in writing from the publisher. Infringers of copyright render themselves liable to prosecution.

ISBN 0 7900 0681 2
First published 1999

©1999 Brian Gill — text
©1999 Geoff Moon — photographs

The authors assert their moral rights in the work.

All photographs by Geoff Moon except those credited otherwise.
Designed by Sunny H. Yang
Edited by Carolyn Lagahetau

Printed in Hong Kong

contents

Preface 9

Introduction 11

What is Endemism? 11

Enumerating New Zealand's Endemic Birds 12

Regional Endemism within New Zealand 13

Classification and Arrangement 13

Origin of New Zealand Birds 14

Characteristics of the New Zealand Avifauna 15

Vulnerability of New Zealand Birds 17

Extinct Birds 17

Extinction 18

Causes of Extinction of New Zealand Birds 18

Prehistoric Distributions 19

Outlying Islands 19

New Zealand Bird Superlatives 20

Progress of Ornithology in New Zealand, 1769—1968 21

New Zealand Bird Books 22

Part One Endemic Species 23

Ratites 24
   Moas 25
   Kiwis 30

Fowl-like Birds 34
   Grouse, Pheasants, Turkeys and Quails 34

Duck-like Birds 36
   Swans, Geese and Ducks 36

Grebes 46

Penguins 48

Tube-nosed Seabirds 52
    Shearwaters, Fulmars, Prions and Petrels 52
    Albatrosses and Mollymawks 60
Pelicans, Gannets, Cormorants and Allies 63
    Cormorants and Shags 63
    Pelicans 68
Herons, Ibises, Storks and Allies 69
    Herons and Bitterns 69
Diurnal Birds of Prey 70
    Hawks and Eagles 70
    Falcons 72
Rails, Cranes and Allies 74
    Adzebills 74
    Rails, Gallinules and Coots 75
Waders, Gulls and Allies 81
    Sandpipers and Snipes 81
    Oystercatchers 83
    Stilts and Avocets 85
    Plovers, Dotterels and Lapwings 87
    Gulls and Terns 93
Pigeons and Doves 96
Parrots and Cockatoos 99
    Parrots and Lorikeets 99
Cuckoos and Allies 106
Owls 108
    Typical Owls 108
Frogmouths and Nightjars 109
    Owlet-nightjars 109
Passerine Birds 110
    New Zealand Wrens 110
    Piopio 117
    Pardalotes, Acanthizid Warblers and Allies 118
    Honeyeaters 120
    Australo-Papuan Robins 126
    Whistlers and Allies 130
    New Zealand Wattlebirds 133
    Crows 138
    Old World Warblers 138

Part Two Other Native Birds 143

Swans, Geese and Ducks 145
Grebes 146
Penguins 147
Shearwaters, Fulmars, Prions and Petrels 148
Albatrosses and Mollymawks 151
Storm Petrels 151
Gannets and Boobies 152
Cormorants and Shags 153
Herons and Bitterns 154
Ibises and Spoonbills 156
Hawks and Eagles 157
Rails, Gallinules and Coots 158
Sandpipers and Snipes 161
Oystercatchers 163
Stilts and Avocets 164
Plovers, Dotterels and Lapwings 165
Gulls and Terns 166
Parrots and Lorikeets 169
Cuckoos and Allies 170
Typical Owls 171
Forest Kingfishers 172
Fantails and Allies 173
Wagtails and Pipits 174
Swallows and Martins 175
White-eyes 176

Appendices
Table One The 37 Genera of Birds Endemic to New Zealand 177
Table Two The 120 Species of Birds Endemic to the New Zealand Region 178
Table Three Species of New Zealand Birds Endemic to Certain Islands 181
Table Four The 34 Endemic Subspecies of New Zealand Birds (belonging to species not endemic) 182

Index 183

Preface

Reed Publishing (NZ) Ltd approached one of us (Geoff) to assemble photographs for a new book on New Zealand birds, and invited the other (Brian) to write the text for it. There are so many books in print (or recently out of print) covering New Zealand birds photographically, that we were keen to pursue a different slant on the subject. We eventually settled on the idea of dealing primarily with the endemic species — the birds unique to New Zealand — and the greater part of this book covers these to give them the emphasis they deserve. The other native birds are treated more briefly. In the text we have attempted to summarise and encapsulate what is most interesting or notable about each endemic species, without repeating too many general details of distribution and life history that are easily found in other books.

The illustrations in this book have all been reproduced from transparencies taken in New Zealand. None of the photographs have, in any way, been altered or enhanced by digital manipulation.

We wish to acknowledge the following people for their assistance in producing this book: Ray Richards for acting as our agent at the start of the project; Peter Janssen and Carolyn Lagahetau of Reed Publishing (NZ) Ltd for seeing the book through to production; Sunny Yang for the design; Dr Ralph Powlesland for reading the text at draft stage and suggesting many improvements, and Brian O'Flaherty for his copy-editing on Reed's behalf.

Brian Gill and Geoff Moon
Auckland, New Zealand

Introduction

The endemic birds of an area — those originating there and found in the wild nowhere else — are always of special interest. *New Zealand's Unique Birds* looks at the endemic birds of New Zealand, both living and extinct, and concentrates on the features that make them unique or interesting. Among New Zealand's unique birds we find, for example, such species as the world's largest living rail and largest living parrot. Among the extinct species were the world's tallest bird, biggest penguin, biggest eagle and biggest owlet-nightjar.

New Zealand is a 'centre of endemism' — a region where the relative proportion of endemic species is high. There are two main reasons. Firstly, New Zealand is an ancient land in the sense that for more than 80 million years it has carried a varied and unique assemblage of plants and animals. This is in contrast to the situation in northern Europe and the British Isles, for example, where the advance of ice sheets during the ice ages periodically displaced many of the animals and plants. Those that returned to Britain and Europe after the last ice age, 15,000 years ago, were widespread Eurasian species. Meanwhile, New Zealand kept an ancient biota, even though at times it was limited to small areas of refuge.

Secondly, New Zealand represents a natural experiment on a grand scale. If the mammals of the world had died out along with the dinosaurs 65 million years ago, and if birds had thus come to dominate the terrestrial habitats unchallenged, how would birds have evolved? The development of New Zealand birds in the absence of mammals has given answers to questions like these, and yielded a bird fauna rich in endemic species.

This book deals primarily with the 120 species of New Zealand endemic birds that have survived into the late twentieth century or that have died out relatively recently, within the last 600 years or so. All these birds were known to the Maori people. The first of them — the Spotted Shag, Weka and Bellbird — became known to Europeans when they were described and named in 1786. Fossil birds that died out before people reached New Zealand are not covered in this book.

WHAT is Endemism?

The bird fauna of a region consists of native species (occurring there naturally) and introduced species (deliberately or accidentally introduced by people). The native birds are further divisible into the endemics (those found nowhere else; see Part One) and the non-endemics (native but found elsewhere as well; see Part Two). In this book the main focus (Part One) is on the endemic species unique to New Zealand, like the Paradise Shelduck and the Tui, rather than those that occur in other countries and are merely New Zealand natives, like the Pukeko and the New Zealand Kingfisher. Part Two of the text gives a brief overview of the most common or notable non-endemic native birds, with an emphasis on mainland species.

Endemic animals or plants are found only in a particular geographic area. The word 'endemic' (in this context) is meaningless without reference to a region. Ultimately, every animal is endemic — even the most widely distributed species — for life as we know it is endemic to earth. However, the term is usually used at the opposite end of the spectrum with reference to species with limited distributions, especially those on islands.

As well as birds never found beyond New Zealand, it is convenient to regard as endemic those birds that breed only in New Zealand but which occur elsewhere in a non-breeding capacity. Royal Albatrosses, Banded Dotterels and Long-tailed Cuckoos breed only in New Zealand, but the albatross ranges widely in the southern oceans, a proportion of the dotterel population migrates to Australia outside the breeding season, and during the New Zealand winter the cuckoo is found in a huge arc of islands across the south-west Pacific. They are still treated as New Zealand endemics for the purposes of this book.

Some species narrowly miss out on being New Zealand endemics. The White-fronted Tern (*Sterna striata*), would have a major entry in this book if a few did not breed on some of the Australian Bass Strait islands. The White-naped Petrel (*Pterodroma cervicalis*), was thought to be extinct until 1969, when it was found breeding at Macauley Island in the Kermadec group. It is not a New Zealand endemic because it was recently found breeding in small numbers on Norfolk Island, and there is a suspicion it breeds in Vanuatu.

Norfolk Island is a problem because it is biogeographically a part of the New Zealand region but politically a part of Australia. An arbitrary decision has been made to include in this book species currently endemic to New Zealand even though they may formerly have bred on Norfolk, and/or Lord Howe, Islands. Pycroft's Petrel, for example, once bred on both Norfolk and Lord Howe, but as a breeder it is now confined to New Zealand.

ENUMERATING New Zealand's Endemic Birds

Endemism can be discussed at different taxonomic levels. It may be that a subspecies is endemic to a certain area, or perhaps a whole species is. An entire genus (containing one or more species) may be endemic to an island or country, or endemism may extend to a family (containing one or more genera) or to an order (containing one or more families). The higher the taxonomic group the less likely it is to be endemic to a restricted area.

Highest-level Endemics

Among the New Zealand land vertebrates (amphibians, reptiles, birds and mammals), the tuataras (*Sphenodon punctatus* and *S. guntheri*) constitute an endemic order (Sphenodontida). This is one of the four orders into which the living reptiles of the world are divided, making tuataras exceptionally interesting. The moas and kiwis are sometimes put in orders of their own (Dinornithiformes and Apterygiformes respectively), both endemic to New Zealand, but in this book the two groups are treated as members of the order Struthioniformes (containing all the ratite birds). However, under the latter arrangement, the moas constitute an endemic suborder. There is some suggestion that the adzebills (*Aptornis*) may be endemic at about the same level as the moas, but more work is needed on this issue. The New Zealand wrens (Acanthisittidae) are also endemic at a level between family and order.

Family-level Endemics

At the level of the taxonomic family (family names end in -idae), the New Zealand native frogs (*Leiopelma*) have their own endemic family (Leiopelmatidae). Since the tuataras are an endemic order they must be an endemic family as well (Sphenodontidae). Among New Zealand birds there are seven endemic families:

- Emeidae (emeid moas);
- Dinornithidae (dinornithid moas);
- Apterygidae (kiwis);
- Aptornithidae (adzebills);
- Acanthisittidae (New Zealand wrens);
- Turnagridae (piopios);
- Callaeidae (New Zealand wattlebirds).

Among mammals, there is a family of bats unique to New Zealand (Mystacinidae).

Genus-level Endemics

As things stand, currently there are reckoned to be 37 endemic genera of New Zealand birds (listed in Table One, page 177). However, this listing is unstable. In recent years, for example, the genera *Megaegotheles*, *Finschia* and *Thinornis*, which used to be reserved for New Zealand species, have lost their status as endemic genera. Published studies showed that the single species in each of the first two genera were not distinct enough to warrant a genus of their own. *Thinornis* ceased to be an endemic genus when an Australian species was transferred to it. Further such changes are inevitable. New studies could either decrease or increase the number of endemic genera.

Species-level Endemics

Table Two (page 178) lists the 120 species of birds considered endemic to New Zealand for the purposes of this book. This list, as with that of endemic genera (Table One), will not prove stable, mainly because opinion changes on whether certain birds are species or subspecies. Where two closely related birds live in the same area, yet do not interbreed and lose their identities, clearly they are distinct species. A perennial problem is whether closely related birds occupying separate areas represent different species or are merely geographic races of the same species. Where related birds are separated geographically, rather arbitrary decisions must be made about their status, and opinions may change.

To take a few examples, the Chatham Island Oystercatcher, *Haematopus chathamensis*, is here treated as a full species following the *New Zealand Checklist* (Turbott, E.G. [convener] 1990. *Checklist of the Birds of New Zealand and the Ross Dependency, Antarctica*. 3rd ed. Random Century, Auckland), but it is not very distinctive and was originally described as only subspecifically different from the South Island Pied Oystercatcher, *Haematopus ostralegus*, of mainland New Zealand. The New Zealand Quail is now regarded as a full species, but until recently it was usually regarded as a subspecies of the Stubble Quail of Australia. Many North and South Island pairs (geese, adzebills, takahes, *Pachyplichas* wrens) could be species or subspecies pairs. Even the Yellowhead and Whitehead, so different in size, colour and behaviour, were once regarded as subspecies.

Opinions can shift back and forward on such issues because there are arguments on both sides. At present we are in a 'splitting' phase with a tendency to regard a good many distinguishable forms as full species.

Endemics at the Subspecific Level

Endemic subspecies are covered briefly in Part Two (see also Table Four, page 182). In this book the emphasis is on endemic species rather than endemic subspecies. Species are a product of our classifying minds, but however hard some of them are to recognise or diagnose, in theory they have a counterpart in the real world. Subspecies, or geographic races, tend to be more arbitrary.

REGIONAL Endemism within New Zealand

Some endemic species are widespread, but others are limited to certain of the islands within the New Zealand archipelago (Table Three, page 181). The South Island has eighteen endemic species of its own, followed by the Chatham group with seventeen, the North Island with ten and the Subantarctic Islands with eight. Stewart Island has no endemic species. The larger size of the South Island and its greater altitudinal variation probably account for the development there of more endemics than on the North Island. The Chathams were to New Zealand what New Zealand was to Australia — an isolated, off-lying centre of endemism — and the large number of Chatham Island endemics is not surprising.

CLASSIFICATION and Arrangement

Quite apart from the problems of deciding where species begin and end, are the problems of how to arrange and classify them in a meaningful way. The ideal is to have related species grouped together so that each family and order is 'monophyletic' — it contains the species resulting from a single evolutionary line. It is undesirable to group the products of two or more evolutionary lines. They are not truly related (they are a 'polyphyletic' group), however confusingly similar they may appear. In a written list of birds you would want to put the groups first that are thought to be more 'primitive' in the sense that their evolutionary lines diverged earliest from the mainstream. The most 'advanced' or recently derived groups would come last in the list.

For many decades, up to the 1980s, a particular arrangement of the higher groups of birds had been traditional. This arrangement placed kiwis, grebes, tube-nosed seabirds and penguins near the start of the sequence, passerines at the end, and rails, cranes, waders and gulls at about the middle. The arrangement reflected accumulated data on the morphology of birds (including their bones and other structures, internal and external) and on their behaviour. Then scientists began looking at biochemical characters (such as the nature of egg-white proteins) to see if these could give objective indications of the relationships of birds. Techniques have also been developed to study the chemical behaviour of strands of DNA, the genetic material itself. These studies of the molecular biology of birds, especially the DNA work, have sometimes supported traditional ideas of which bird groups are most closely related, and other times suggested radically new relationships. Accepting all the results of the DNA studies has led to a very unorthodox rearrangement of the higher bird groups, which many people are following. However, it is most unlikely that biochemistry alone can produce the final word on bird relationships. What molecular biology yields up is just another taxonomic character to be weighed against all others.

In this book the species of birds and their Latin and common names are largely as set down in the last edition of the *New Zealand Checklist* (Turbott 1990). However, there are various departures flowing from the results of new studies published after 1990. Following the lead of other publications, the sequence of bird species and their arrangement in higher categories has been partly modified from that of the *Checklist* following an important new listing of Australian birds (Christidis, L. and Boles, W.E. *The Taxonomy and Species of Birds of Australia and its Territories*. R.A.O.U., Melbourne, 1994). This listing takes the sensible approach of accepting the latest DNA findings when they are corroborated by other data. The order of birds in the present book therefore departs a little from the traditional.

One of the exciting things about birds is that they are the best-known animal group. It seems that, for the first time, we are getting tantalisingly close to working out the actual evolutionary family-tree ('phylogeny') of an entire animal group.

ORIGIN of New Zealand Birds

The theory of continental drift, and the idea that the continents were once joined together to form 'supercontinents', is now widely accepted. The islands we call New Zealand were once joined to the other Southern Hemisphere landmasses in a supercontinent named Gondwana (after a region in India of the same name where important rocks relating to the supercontinent were found). New Zealand broke away from this giant continent 80–85 million years ago, as the Tasman Sea formed between New Zealand and Australia. This made difficult the spread to New Zealand of any more animals that could not swim, float or fly.

The break-up of Gondwana caused New Zealand, now about 2000 km from Australia, to become the most isolated landmass of its size. All larger landmasses are less isolated, and the more isolated islands are smaller. New Zealand lies well out in the Pacific Ocean, which is the world's largest geographic feature. The Pacific comprises nearly a third of the earth's surface, and essentially we are a speck of land in what is almost a water hemisphere. Isolation is the dominant theme in the origin and evolution of New Zealand birds.

Isolation has limited the spread of land birds to New Zealand, and prevented snakes and land mammals from spreading here of their own accord (or recolonising, if they ever were here but died out). Though an isolated group of islands, New Zealand was large enough that the formation of new species could to some extent proceed within the country by the geographic separation of populations, as takes place on continents. What our land birds lack in numbers is made up for by the interest that attaches to them for having evolved for so long in such isolation.

Because New Zealand is small it is statistically unlikely that any major group of animals arose here and spread to colonise other areas. We assume that New Zealand was colonised from time to time by animals that had arisen elsewhere. The ancestors of some birds arrived before New Zealand broke with Gondwana, or soon after. These are often survivors of lineages that died out in other parts of the world, and their descendants now seem 'primitive' or 'ancient'. The moas are examples. Other birds descend from populations that colonised New Zealand (mainly from the west) by crossing the sea at various times in the last 80–85 million years. In general, the more closely related our birds are to those elsewhere, the more recently they arrived. The process of colonisation continues, and some of our commonest native birds today began as stragglers from Australia a few decades ago (see Part Two).

It used to be thought that Australia, and hence to a major degree New Zealand, received its modern bird groups as colonisers from south-east Asia. It is now becoming clear that the Southern Hemisphere, and indeed Australia itself, were important centres for the origin of various bird groups. It seems likely that at least five major groups — grebes, ducks, pigeons, parrots and passerines — arose in the Southern Hemisphere and did not spread to the Northern Hemisphere until about 25 million years ago. Though increasingly isolated by the widening of the Tasman Sea during the last 80–85 million years, New Zealand was at the edge of a major centre of bird evolution and was able to share in the adaptive radiation of some major groups of birds.

Double Invasions

Among New Zealand terrestrial birds there are pairs of closely related species in which one member of the pair is either larger, or less able to fly, or darker, or a combination of these characteristics. These pairs of species represent double invasions of New Zealand by the same ancestral stock. The descendants of the earlier invasions evolved into distinct species which, in the absence of snakes and mammalian predators, sometimes became larger and less adept at flying. The second invasion was often so recent that the descendants are little different from their relatives in Australia. Double invasion has been an important mechanism for generating new species among New Zealand birds. It is speciation by the separation of populations in *time*. In continents it is more usual for speciation to be by the separation of populations in *space* (geographically).

The pairs of species most likely to represent double invasions (with the result of the earlier invasion given first) are:

- Weka — Banded Rail
- Takahes (two species) — Pukeko
- Black Stilt — Pied Stilt
- Antipodes Island Parakeet — Red-crowned Parakeet
- New Zealand Robin — New Zealand Tomtit

The double invasion of parakeets pertains only to the Antipodes Islands; the others relate to the mainland. The Black and Pied Stilts are of similar size, while in the other four pairs of species the first-named is much larger. The first-named species are the less colourful of the pairs, with the Black Stilt a melanistic extreme. The Banded Rail, Pukeko and Pied Stilt are species that occur also in Australia (and elsewhere). The Red-crowned Parakeet of the Antipodes is the same species that occurs on mainland New Zealand. The New Zealand Tomtit is a New Zealand endemic but it has close relatives of the same small size in Australia.

Other pairs that perhaps stem from double invasions (result of earlier invasion first) are:

- Moas — Kiwis
- Dieffenbach's Rail — Banded Rail
- Chatham Island Rail — Banded Rail
- Hodgen's Rail — Black-tailed Native-hen
- Giant Coots (two species) — Eurasian Coot
- Giant Chatham Island Snipe — Chatham Island Snipe
- New Zealand Dotterel — Banded Dotterel
- Kakapo — Kaka and Kea
- Laughing Owl — Morepork
- Chatham Island Warbler — Grey Warbler

The first of the pair is larger except for the Chatham Island Rail, which is smaller. The Black-tailed Native-hen is a rare vagrant to New Zealand.

CHARACTERISTICS of the New Zealand Avifauna

New Zealand's bird fauna is dominated by three main elements: the unique land birds, the tube-nosed seabirds and the migratory waders. The members of the first group are the product of isolation, but this has been no impediment to the seabirds and waders.

New Zealand is a mecca and refuge for the oceanic seabirds (albatrosses, petrels and other procellariiforms) which range widely at sea to feed but must find land on which to nest. Approximately two-thirds of the world's species of tube-nosed seabirds are found in Australian and New Zealand waters. New Zealand has a greater diversity of these birds than any other country of a similar size, and the numbers of individuals are astounding. About 2.8 million pairs of Sooty Shearwaters breed at the tiny Snares Islands, 300 km south of Invercargill. This is said to be more procellariiforms than nest in all the British Isles (partly reflecting the relative unimportance of these birds in Britain as in many other Northern Hemisphere countries).

Similarly, isolation has been irrelevant for the charadriiform wading birds, many of which are long-distance migrants. Numerous species of waders breed in the Northern Hemisphere and spend the northern winter benefiting from New Zealand's summertime abundance of food. Certain of these transequatorial migrants arrive in such great numbers that they are ecologically important. Some of our waders migrate shorter distances across the Tasman Sea or within New Zealand, and a few are sedentary.

Flightlessness and Gigantism

All birds (and only birds among contemporary animals) have feathers, and certain feathers make flight possible. Flightlessness in birds is therefore ironical, because it is almost a definition of birds that they fly.

Dinosaurs and pterosaurs died out 65 million years ago, and the mammals and birds then diversified to become the co-dominant vertebrate animals on land. For 65 million years birds have dominated the skies during daytime, with bats and various nocturnal birds taking over at night. Birds specialised in being lightly built and able to fly, partly so they could escape from predatory ground-dwelling mammals. Flight has also conferred ease of dispersal to the extent that birds have colonised more parts of the earth's land surface than have reptiles or mammals.

Despite the advantages of flight, some birds have returned to a flightless ground-dwelling condition. It is a 'return' because all flightless birds are secondarily so — they have descended from ancestors that flew.

Flightlessness is found to the greatest extent among the birds of isolated, predator-free islands, that is, they no longer need to fly to escape predators. Flying demands a great deal of energy and the ability to fly is lost very quickly when it is no longer needed. New Zealand is renowned for its large number of flightless birds. This number is so large simply because New Zealand lacked predatory mammals until the arrival of humans, about 1000 years ago.

Flightlessness is characteristic of the ratite birds, the New Zealand examples of which are the moas and kiwis. Another group, the rails (family Rallidae), is remarkable for the frequency and speed with which its members have become flightless on predator-free islands all around the world. New Zealand has several flightless rails. Flightlessness among the perching (passerine) birds is exceedingly rare, and New Zealand has the only examples known: the Stephens Island Wren, Yaldwyn's Wren, Grant-Mackie's Wren and the Long-billed Wren.

The only predators of birds in primaeval New Zealand were other birds such as owls, raptors, skuas, gulls and kingfishers. Under these circumstances many New Zealand birds became flightless, while others are weak fliers showing signs of development in the direction of flightlessness.

In many cases large size developed with the loss of flight, and several New Zealand birds are giant forms, bigger than all, or most, of their nearest relatives. The following are all 'giants' in this sense: the Giant Moa, New Zealand Eagle, Weka, Giant Chatham Island Rail, South Island Takahe, Chatham Island Coot, Giant Chatham Island Snipe, Kakapo, New Zealand Owlet-nightjar, and the New Zealand Robin.

Dullness and Melanism

New Zealand's endemic birds tend to be drab, some to the extent that they are black. The best examples are the Snares Islands subspecies of the New Zealand Tomtit and the Black Robin, both of which have totally black plumage. Adult pure-bred Black Stilts are completely melanistic, unlike their young. The Huia was black except for the white tail-tip. The Variable Oystercatcher has a black colour form. The New Zealand Fantail has a black colour form in New Zealand that is lacking in populations of the same species in Australia and elsewhere. The New Zealand Robin is almost completely dark grey. New Zealand parrots are dull-coloured as parrots go and the Tui is among the darkest of honeyeaters.

Why such a number of New Zealand birds should be dull or dark is not known. For birds of more than one colour, it may be that in New Zealand's isolated and largely predator-free environment, the natural selection that normally maintains countershading and disruptive patterns for camouflage was relaxed. In some cases it could also be that having become longer-lived and slower-breeding, birds had less need for advertisement and display within populations and between species.

Bergmann's Rule

This rule states that where birds and mammals vary geographically, body-size tends to be larger among the populations in cooler areas; that is, towards the south in New Zealand's case (or in the direction of higher altitude).

Several New Zealand birds tend to be smaller in the North Island than in the South Island in agreement with Bergmann's Rule. This is so, for example, in the *Dinornis* moas, the extinct geese (*Cnemiornis* spp.), the adzebills (*Aptornis* spp.), the New Zealand Owlet-nightjar, the Kaka and the extinct wrens of the genus *Pachyplichas*. However, Bergmann's Rule is not universal among New Zealand birds. There is evidence from the following species of smaller size towards the south: the last populations of the Upland Moa during the past 10,000 years, the takahes (*Porphyrio* spp.) and Stewart Island Wekas versus the nominate race from western areas of the South Island.

Communal Breeding

Communal breeding takes place when individuals additional to the breeding pair help to feed and defend nestlings and fledglings. The helpers are usually the breeding pair's own young from a previous breeding season. They are thus helping their own parents and siblings. This means that their seemingly selfless behaviour is in fact directed at promoting the success of their own genes in the next best way to producing young of their own.

Communal breeding is rare in most temperate areas of the world, but is now known to be a feature of many birds of the Australasian region. It was largely overlooked until the 1970s, and the factors that encourage it are unclear. New Zealand birds now known to be communal breeders are the Pukeko, Rifleman, Whitehead, Yellowhead and the Brown Creeper.

VULNERABILITY of New Zealand Birds

When New Zealand broke from the rest of Gondwana, mammals and snakes — the main predators of birds today — had not yet spread throughout the supercontinent, or if they reached New Zealand they later died out. New Zealand therefore escaped colonisation by land mammals (other than bats) until the arrival of man, and remains one of the few temperate areas lacking land snakes.

As well as becoming large and flightless, another peculiarity of birds on predator-free islands is that their reproductive rate slows down. They live long lives, and rear few young slowly. This is in contrast to successful continental birds like the House Sparrow (*Passer domesticus*), where life in the 'fast lane' has selected birds that raise large families quickly at almost any time of year.

In short, the characteristics of many New Zealand birds were such that the arrival of land mammals, as on other oceanic islands, was catastrophic. During the last 1000 years the ancient bird fauna of New Zealand has been greatly reduced. As a contrast, the colonisation of Australia by Europeans in the last 200 years, and the introduction during that time of cats, foxes and more rats, had relatively little impact on a bird fauna already co-existing with snakes, predatory mammals and Aborigines, the last having been in Australia for perhaps 60,000 years.

EXTINCT Birds

In discussing New Zealand's endemic birds we must unfortunately dwell on extinction. Of the 120 endemic species, 40 percent (48) are now extinct (see Table Two). Of the 37 endemic genera, 54 percent (20) are now extinct (see Table One). These extinctions are due to the ecological disruption caused by the presence of people in New Zealand, which began about 1000 years ago, and continues to the present. Those birds, like the adzebills, which died out after Maori settlement but before European settlement, are known mainly from bones preserved in young fossil deposits or in kitchen middens. Those like the Huia, which became extinct after the arrival of Europeans about 200 years ago, are known mainly from mounted specimens, study skins and eggs collected for museums when the species still lived.

New Zealand lost 37 species of birds (a third of its endemic species) during the 800 years between the arrival of Polynesians and Europeans in New Zealand. The losses included the 'megafauna' — all sixteen species over 10 kg in weight (the eleven moas, the adzebills, the New Zealand Eagle and the New Zealand geese). In historical times (the last 200 years) we lost another eleven species.

There are also about a score of bird species that frequented New Zealand 1–40 million years ago, which we know from completely fossilised bones (which geological forces have turned to stone). In nearly every case we have only fragments of the skeleton, from which very little can be deduced about the details of the birds' outward appearances. Most of these birds are penguins, New Zealand being a major site for fossil penguins. Among them is the world's largest penguin, the New Zealand Giant Penguin, *Pachydyptes ponderosus*, which stood about 1.5 m tall and may have weighed over 100 kg. These species are excluded from this book which deals only with the birds living when New Zealand was first settled by humans.

EXTINCTION

Every species becomes extinct in the long run. Some simply die out and their evolutionary line reaches a dead end. This is believed to have been the case with nearly all the dinosaurs, for example, which abruptly disappeared from the fossil record at the end of the Cretaceous period about 65 million years ago. But other species have become extinct as their descendants have evolved into one or more new species differing significantly from their ancestors. It seems likely that a species of dinosaur gave rise to birds; it can only have been one species if modern birds share an immediate common ancestor. Thus the dinosaurs are extinct but, if the hypothesis is correct, birds live on as the direct descendants of a particular line of dinosaurs.

Natural though extinction may ultimately be, it is important to recognise that the rate of extinction has been accelerated wherever humans have spread. The extinct birds in this book have been hastened to extinction by the impact of people in New Zealand.

CAUSES of Extinction of New Zealand Birds

For extinctions during the period of human presence in New Zealand, the following are likely contributing factors.

Destruction of Habitat

When Polynesians reached New Zealand 1000 years ago, the country was almost completely forested. Their clearance of the land, especially in the dry, eastern parts of both islands, reduced the forest until it covered only about two-thirds of New Zealand by 1840. European technology allowed the draining of swamps and a dramatically accelerated rate of deforestation. Today, native forest covers only 20 percent of New Zealand, and little of it is richly diverse lowland forest. Many New Zealand birds were specialised forest or swamp dwellers and could not survive such a radical loss of habitat.

Introduction of Mammalian Predators

Maori brought with them the Domestic Dog, *Canis familiaris*, and a south-east Asian rat (the Kiore, *Rattus exulans*), both of which can kill birds. The Kiore, which is an agile climber, eats eggs and can kill chicks and adults up to the size of a small albatross. When rats reach a new area they undergo an 'irruption' whereby their numbers quickly reach plague proportions. They eat all available food and their population collapses before settling at a moderate level in equilibrium with what food remains. As the Kiore spread throughout New Zealand its vanguard was probably an irruptive wave that was immensely destructive to bird populations. Europeans brought with them three more rodents — Ship Rats (*Rattus rattus*), Norway Rats (*R. norvegicus*) and House Mice (*Mus musculus*) — whose spread, like that of the Kiore, would have been preceded by an irruptive wave. The Europeans also introduced Domestic Cats (*Felis catus*), which became feral, and three mustelids: Feral Ferrets (*Mustela furo*), Stoats (*M. erminea*) and Weasels (*M. nivalis*). Many New Zealand birds were unable to cope with predation by these mammals.

Predation by Humans

Maori were heavily dependent on birds as a source of protein, especially during the first 500 years of settlement. Europeans, though less dependent on wild birds for food, introduced guns and so enhanced killing efficiency. Hunting flourished with Victorian and Edwardian collectors, who shot New Zealand birds for museum specimens or the millinery trade.

Climatic and Vegetational Change

Some 10,000 years ago the climate of New Zealand began to warm, and forest slowly colonised subalpine grassland and scrub that had developed over large areas during the ice ages, particularly in the South Island. It has been suggested that this may have reduced the distribution of many of the moas, the adzebills, the geese, the New Zealand Eagle and the New Zealand Crow, all of which may have been adapted to grassland or forest edges. With their populations thus reduced, these birds may have been all the more vulnerable to the three factors given above.

Introduction of Bird Diseases

Europeans successfully acclimatised over 30 species of foreign birds in New Zealand — mainly from Europe — and attempted to introduce many more. When these birds were imported they would have carried with them disease-causing viruses, micro-organisms and parasites. At least some of these diseases must have spread to the native birds, which would have lacked immunity and resistance. Birds that suffered a particularly sudden decline, such as the Laughing Owl and Piopio, may have been affected in this way. Disease is thought to be the most likely explanation for the sudden decline of the Bellbird in settled parts of the North Island in the 1860s. It recovered, except in Northland where it remains locally extinct.

PREHISTORIC Distributions

As expected, from a knowledge of how disruptive humans have been, it can be seen that the distributions of New Zealand birds before Maori and European settlement were very different from present distributions. Fortunately there is a fossil record from which some knowledge of the past can be reconstructed. Unmineralised 'subfossil' bones are recovered from cave silts, dune sands and layers of alkaline mud in swamp deposits. Subfossil bones are little changed from modern bones. They are mostly between a few hundred and 10,000 years old, sometimes older, but never so old that they have become petrified by geological forces. The term 'subfossil' is regarded as undefinable by some researchers who prefer the term 'Holocene fossil', the Holocene (or Postglacial) Epoch being the last 10,000 years.

Other important sources of data on prehistoric distributions are the bird bones among the faunal remains recovered by archaeologists from Maori and Moriori kitchen middens. These bones are younger than 1000 years, and strictly speaking they are not fossils since they were not buried naturally. Archaeological records show that Maori people relied heavily on wild birds for food until about 500 years ago, by which time moas and certain other birds had been eliminated. Smaller forest birds, fish and shellfish then became relatively more important foods.

The evidence from Holocene fossils and archaeological sites usually shows that endemic birds that are rare today had much wider distributions in the recent past.

OUTLYING Islands

New Zealand is an archipelago. Within 60 km of the three main islands (North, South and Stewart) there are around 650 'offshore' islands and islets. More distantly, New Zealand (as politically defined) encompasses seven 'outlying' island groups, details of which follow. The offshore and outlying islands have fostered the development of endemic species and subspecies, and since the arrival of humans have acted as refuges for numerous endemic species that otherwise would not have survived.

The Kermadec Islands

These are about 1000 km north-east of Auckland at the edge of the subtropics. Several tropical seabirds breed there that do not otherwise breed in the New Zealand region, but there are no endemic bird species.

The Chatham Islands

The Chatham group is 860 km east of Christchurch. It is the next largest part of New Zealand after Stewart Island (excluding the Ross Dependency). The main island (Chatham Island itself) covers about 90,000 ha, much of it a huge lagoon. A distinctive bird fauna developed on the Chatham Islands, and nine endemic species survive today: two petrels that breed nowhere else (Chatham Petrel, Magenta Petrel); and two shags (Chatham Island Shag, Pitt Island Shag), two charadriiforms (Chatham Island Oystercatcher, Chatham Island Snipe), a pigeon (Chatham Island Pigeon) and two songbirds (Chatham Island Warbler, Black Robin) that occur nowhere else. No moa remains have been found on the Chatham Islands.

Polynesians, probably from New Zealand, settled the Chatham Islands within the last 1000 years. They cleared forest by burning and introduced the Kiore. European settlement brought further ecological disruption.

Of New Zealand's 48 extinct birds, eight species (Chatham Island Duck, Chatham Island Sea-eagle, Chatham Island Rail, Dieffenbach's Rail, Giant Chatham Island Rail, Chatham Island Coot, Giant Chatham Island Snipe, and the Chatham Island Fernbird) were unique to the Chathams. Thus the group has lost 47 percent of its endemic birds, and contributed disproportionately for its size to the list of extinct birds of New Zealand.

The Subantarctic Islands

New Zealand administers five groups of Subantarctic Islands which are, from north to south: Bounty, Snares, Antipodes, Auckland and Campbell Islands. The closest is the Snares group (100 km south-west of Stewart Island) and the most distant is the Antipodes group (about 800 km south-east of Stewart Island). They are characterised by strong winds, cool temperatures, vegetation of a subalpine character, and the presence of penguins and both burrowing and surface-nesting procellariiform seabirds. There was no prehistoric Maori settlement, but whalers and sealers had a major impact in the early 1800s. There are eight species endemic to the New Zealand Subantarctic Islands (see Table Three, page 181).

NEW ZEALAND Bird Superlatives

These are some of the ways in which New Zealand's endemic birds are remarkable.

- **Moas** — the only wingless birds.
- **Coastal Moa** — the smallest moa (c. 20 kg).
- **Giant Moa** — the tallest bird (3 m); the largest New Zealand bird (up to 270 kg).
- **Kiwis** — the only birds with nostrils at the end of the bill.
- **Little Spotted Kiwi** — the smallest ratite bird; lays one of the largest eggs of any bird (relative to female size, 23 percent).
- **Auckland Island Merganser** — the smallest merganser.
- **Royal Albatross** — the largest seabird (with Wandering Albatross, c. 9 kg); has the greatest wingspan of any bird (with Wandering Albatross, 3.5 m); the only albatross nesting on the mainland; has the longest incubation period of any bird (with Wandering Albatross, often over 80 days); the longest-lived New Zealand wild bird (over 50 years).
- **New Zealand Eagle** — the largest bird of prey.
- **Snipe-rail** — has the longest bill of any rail (relative to head-size).
- **South Island Takahe** — the largest living rail (c. 3 kg).
- **Variable Oystercatcher** — the only oystercatcher with colour forms.
- **Black Stilt** — the only entirely black stilt.
- **Wrybill** — the only bird with a beak curved to one side.
- **Kakapo** — the heaviest parrot (males c. 2.5 kg); the parrot with the greatest weight difference between the sexes; the only flightless parrot; the only 'lek'-breeder among parrots, flightless birds and New Zealand birds.
- **New Zealand Owlet-nightjar** — the largest owlet-nightjar.
- **Rifleman** — the smallest New Zealand bird (total length c. 80 mm, weight c. 6.5 g).
- **Stephens Island Wren** — the only flightless passerine bird (with three other extinct New Zealand wrens).
- **Grey Warbler** — lays one of the largest eggs of any bird (relative to female size, 23 percent).
- **Stitchbird** — the only living honeyeater that nests in tree-holes.
- **Huia** — the bill of the male and female differ more radically in shape than in any other bird.
- **New Zealand Crow** — the largest New Zealand passerine bird.

PROGRESS of Ornithology in New Zealand, *1769–1968*

Ornithology (the study of birds) has developed steadily in New Zealand, and the following are some of the dates and events during the 200 years beginning 1769 that are ornithologically significant.

1769–77: Three voyages of Captain James Cook to New Zealand. Naturalists on board collected specimens and made paintings from which about 60 species of birds in the New Zealand region were later validly described.

1786: First published species descriptions of endemic New Zealand birds (Spotted Shag, Weka and Bellbird). Swedishman Anders Sparrman described them in the first instalment of his publication *Museum Carlsonianum*. Sparrman had joined Cook's second voyage, and the birds were collected in Queen Charlotte and Dusky Sounds.

1812: First record of the capture of a kiwi by a European. The stuffed skin was taken to London, creating great interest in scientific circles.

1824–59: British, French, Austrian and American exploring and surveying expeditions visited New Zealand, and some made important bird collections.

1839: The British anatomist, Richard Owen, announced his deduction, from examination of a partial thigh bone, that large ostrich-like birds (what we now call moas) once occurred in New Zealand.

1843: Publication of the first list of New Zealand birds; by G.R. Gray of the British Museum (as an appendix to Ernst Dieffenbach's book *Travels in New Zealand*).

1873: Publication of the first edition of Sir Walter Buller's *A History of the Birds of New Zealand*.

1910: Publication of *Birds of the Water, Wood and Waste*, first of five books by W.H. Guthrie-Smith (the last in 1936) containing pioneering photographs of New Zealand birds. In similar vein was *Life Histories of New Zealand Birds* by E.F. Stead (1932). Such photographic books proliferated after World War II.

1923: Formation of the Native Bird Protection Society (later the Royal Forest and Bird Protection Society) to promote the conservation of wildlife and habitats.

1930: Publication of the first edition of *New Zealand Birds* by W.R.B. Oliver, a comprehensive account of the New Zealand avifauna.

1940: (1) Formation of the Ornithological Society of New Zealand. The society publishes a quarterly periodical (*Notornis*, originally *New Zealand Bird Notes*) which contains results of studies of New Zealand birds, and operates schemes to record the nesting, storm-wrecking, distribution, numbers and moult of birds. (2) Submission of the first M.Sc. thesis on birds by a student at a New Zealand university ('The systematics, distribution, bionomics and some aspects of the anatomy of the genus *Pachyptila* Illiger', by C.A. Fleming, University of Auckland). University theses have since become a major outlet for research on New Zealand birds.

1945: Establishment of a Wildlife Branch (within the Department of Internal Affairs), which later became the New Zealand Wildlife Service and merged with other organisations in 1987 to become the Department of Conservation. These government departments have carried out significant research on New Zealand birds, as did the Ecology Division of the Department of Scientific and Industrial Research from the mid-1940s to 1992.

1948: Rediscovery of the South Island Takahe near Lake Te Anau, dramatically focusing attention on the need to study and conserve New Zealand's endemic birds.

1950: The Ornithological Society commenced a Nest Record Scheme and established the centralised banding (ringing) scheme for wild birds (other than gamebirds) that is now run by the Department of Conservation. Local, uncoordinated banding of New Zealand birds began in 1911.

1951: (1) Formation of the New Zealand Ecological Society to promote the study of the interrelationships between plants and animals, including birds. (2) Commencement of a Beach Patrol Scheme by the Ornithological Society, to record the incidence of oceanic seabirds washed up dead on beaches, particularly after storms.

1966: Publication of the first modern field guide to New Zealand birds; published by Collins and written by R.A. Falla, R.B. Sibson and E.G. Turbott.

NEW ZEALAND Bird Books

Handbooks

A 'handbook' to the birds of a region provides detailed information about each species, including illustrations, but is usually too big to carry in the field.

The first major book devoted to the birds of New Zealand was the first edition of Sir Walter Buller's *A History of the Birds of New Zealand* (1873). In 1888 there was a second edition (in two volumes) with fresh illustrations. A supplement in two volumes was published in 1905. The coloured plates in both editions, by English artist J.G. Keulemans, were superb, and some have been reproduced so often that they are familiar images more than a century later.

In the early 1900s a compact account of the birds was contained within Hutton and Drummond's *The Animals of New Zealand* (1904, and later editions). A milestone was reached in 1930 with the publication of *New Zealand Birds*, by W.R.B. Oliver, containing detailed accounts of all New Zealand birds, both living and extinct. A much revised and expanded second edition appeared in 1955.

The next major handbook was the *Reader's Digest Complete Book of New Zealand Birds* (1985; edited by C.J.R. Robertson), containing text and a coloured photograph for every New Zealand bird. The most detailed account of the birds of New Zealand is (or will be) found in the multi-volume *Handbook of Australian, New Zealand and Antarctic Birds* ('HANZAB'). This monumental work by the Royal Australasian Ornithologists Union in association with Oxford University Press (Australia), gives a highly detailed summary of knowledge for each species. Volumes produced to date are: Volume 1 (Ratites to Ducks; in two parts), Volume 2 (Raptors to Lapwings), Volume 3 (Snipes to Pigeons). The final work will contain six volumes.

Field Guides

Field guides are designed to enable birds to be identified in the field from clear descriptions and pictures (usually paintings that can be contrived to show all the identifying features of a bird). They have to be small enough to be carried easily in a day-pack or car glovebox.

The first New Zealand field guide, though the term was not in use at the time, was Perrine Moncrieff's *New Zealand Birds and How to Identify Them* (1925 and later editions). The first modern field guide, of a type that was becoming known all over the world, was *A Field Guide to the Birds of New Zealand* by Falla, Sibson and Turbott (1966, with several later editions, some under slightly different titles). The latest field guide is *The Field Guide to the Birds of New Zealand* by B.D. Heather and H.A. Robertson (Penguin, 1996).

A field guide to seabirds, *Southern Albatrosses and Petrels — An Identification Guide,* was published in 1978 by Harper and Kinsky. For a photographic field guide to New Zealand birds, see Geoff Moon's *A Field Guide to New Zealand Birds* (Reed, 1992).

Others

Checklists of New Zealand birds, organised by the Ornithological Society of New Zealand and focusing on names of birds and their distribution and status, were published in 1953, 1970 and 1990.

A milestone in ornithological publication was *The Atlas of Bird Distribution in New Zealand* by Bull, Gaze and Robertson (1985), which resulted from a ten-year 'Bird Mapping Scheme' by members of the Ornithological Society.

Two books with historic plates and scholarly text deserve special mention. In 1967 Whitcombe and Tombs reproduced the coloured plates from the second edition of Buller's *A History of the Birds of New Zealand* with excerpts of Buller's text and new text by E.G. Turbott. In 1982, previously unpublished paintings of New Zealand birds by G.E. Lodge appeared with a text by Sir Charles Fleming (*George Edward Lodge — The Unpublished New Zealand Bird Paintings*, Nova Pacifica).

There have been two guides to localities at which to find birds: Ross McKenzie's *In Search of Birds in New Zealand — How and Where to Find Them* (Reed, 1972) and Stuart Chambers' *Birds of New Zealand — Locality Guide* (Arun Books, 1989).

Finally, since World War II, there have been books too numerous to list that have dealt with selections of New Zealand birds, illustrated with superb photographs, paintings and drawings.

A note here on the naming of birds may help some readers with historical interests. Following the Latin name of a bird is sometimes shown the name of the person who first described the species and the year in which the description was published. Brackets around these names and dates indicate that the species was originally placed in a different genus to the one shown. For example, the Little Bush Moa was originally called '*Dinornis didiformis* Owen, 1844'. Later the species was moved to the genus *Anomalopteryx* and so became '*Anomalopteryx didiformis* (Owen, 1844)'.

Part One

Endemic Species

Ratites
(Order STRUTHIONIFORMES)

The ratites are a group of flightless birds few in species but great in importance, because they constitute a major division of the birds. The greatest separation between groups of birds is between the ratites (with only eleven living species) and the non-ratites or carinates (all other birds — nearly 10,000 species). The closest relatives of the ratites are the tinamous — chicken-like birds from Central and South America — that are ground-dwelling but able to fly.

The word ratite is from the Latin *ratis* (raft), and refers to the flat, raft-like breastbone. Carinates, which are mostly flying birds, have a strong keel (carina) on the breastbone for the attachment of their large flight muscles (this keel is easily seen when the breast meat is carved from a roasted chicken). Ratites, on the other hand, are running birds with powerful legs and reduced wings, and their breastbone lacks a keel. They also lack the highly developed vaned feathers of flying birds, and the plumage has an overall shaggy appearance. The palate bones of ratites (and tinamous) have a primitive arrangement not seen in other birds. Male ratites have a well-developed penis (usually lacking in non-ratite birds). Unusually it is the male that plays the greater role in care of the eggs and young.

Ratites occur, or once occurred, on the various landmasses of the Southern Hemisphere. The eleven living ratites are the three species of kiwis (New Zealand), the Emu, *Dromaius novaehollandiae* (Australia), the three cassowaries (Australia and New Guinea), the two ostriches (Africa), and the two rheas (South America). The most notable extinct ratites are the moas of New Zealand and the elephant birds (Family Aepyornithidae) of Madagascar. The seven species of extinct 'giant runners' or 'mihirungs' (Family Dromornithidae) of Australia may be ratites but there is some uncertainty about this.

All ratites have descended from a common ancestor that flew. It used to be thought that moas and kiwis are each other's closest relatives and that they diverged after their common ancestor reached New Zealand. New evidence from studies of DNA, however, suggests that kiwis are more closely related to the Emu and cassowaries than to moas. The evidence also points to the divergence between kiwis and their Australian cousins having occurred at 40–45 million years ago, after the Tasman Sea began to open up about 80 million years ago. If correct, this means that ratites reached New Zealand twice, an early colonisation leading to the moas and a later one to the kiwis. It seems that moas were a primitive group that branched early from the ancestral ratite stock. The ancestor of the moas may have walked to New Zealand while the area was still joined to the supercontinent Gondwana. The ancestral kiwi may have reached New Zealand later, perhaps by 'island-hopping' (there are likely to have been islands at that time in the northern Tasman Sea). It has also been suggested that kiwis descended from an ancestor that flew to New Zealand and became flightless, independent of other ratites.

Moas

Moas are a group of extinct, flightless birds unique to New Zealand. They are the only wingless birds known. Other flightless birds, such as the kiwis and Emu, have reduced wings, but moas had no wings at all. They also lacked the pygostyle, the last bone on the reduced tail of birds. Moas had large, powerful legs. Their necks were also very strong; some neck vertebrae in the Giant Moa are almost as big as those of a horse. The pelvis of moas widens at the rear (in all living ratites it narrows), but the significance of this is not clear. Moas had four toes on each foot; three large toes running forward and a reduced toe facing backwards, as in kiwis.

Moas are known from great numbers of bones, eggshell fragments, a few whole eggs, gizzard stones, feathers and mummified remains with dried tissues and feathers attached. These relics have been recovered from natural sites (sand-dune deposits, cave silts and layers of alkaline mud in swamp deposits) and from some archaeological sites. Taken together, these remains are between a few hundred and a few thousand years old, but there are also a few truly fossilised Pliocene moa bones which are a few million years old.

Moa feathers that have been discovered are up to 18 cm long and have the loose construction typical of the feathers of ratite birds. They would have given moas a 'shaggy' plumage. Moa feathers have a well-developed aftershaft — a secondary feather attached to the main one. Aftershafts occur in some ratites, such as cassowaries, but not in others, like ostriches and kiwis.

Moas swallowed small stones to help to grind their vegetable food in the muscular part of the stomach (the gizzard). Groups of small polished stones, unlike any in the immediate vicinity, are sometimes found along with moa bones. These are gizzard stones or 'gastroliths'.

No more than twenty moa eggs have been found that are sufficiently complete to allow measurement of length or breadth. The eggs are small relative to adult size. Fragments of eggshell are common in both natural deposits and archaeological sites. The outer surface of the moa eggshell is smooth, with round or slit-like pores. Most fragments are cream-coloured. Eggshell fragments are up to 2 mm thick, which is thin when compared with ostrich eggshell.

Measured to the top of the head in an upright standing position, it seems that adult moas of the various species were 1–3 m tall. The smallest adult moas probably weighed 12–15 kg, while the heaviest were estimated to have weighed about

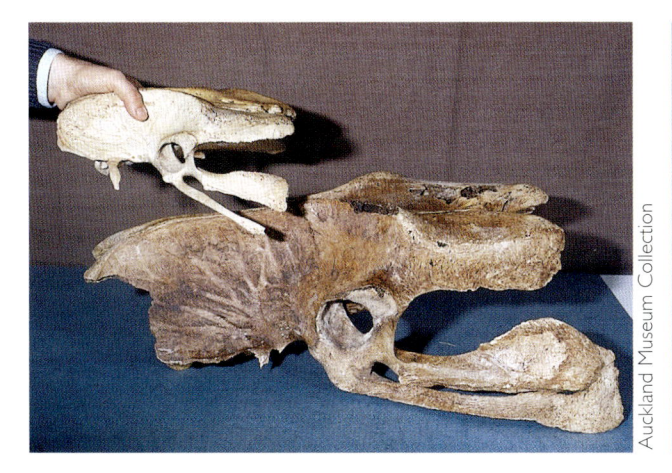

Moa pelves. Larger (below) from Giant Moa, smaller from Coastal Moa.

Moa eggshell fragments from sand-dunes at Tom Bowling Bay, North Cape.

Moa gizzard stones. Larger stones (left) from Slender Bush Moa, smaller stones from Little Bush Moa.

270 kg. Moas differed in overall size, in the maximum height they could reach to browse, in their size and shape of beak, and, no doubt, in their habitat preferences. Thus, several species could co-exist in an area, avoiding competition by exploiting the environment in slightly different ways. Only three species seem to have preferred tall, wet bush — the Little Bush Moa, Slender Bush Moa and the Large Bush Moa. Others preferred drier, less dense forest, shrubland, grassland or the margins where forest met more open country.

Preserved stomach contents in swamp deposits show that moas ate seeds, leaves, stems and green twigs. Moas were browsers of shrubs rather than grazers of grass. They probably had an enlarged caecum, an appendage to the intestine containing bacteria that carried out the breakdown of cellulose to digestible components. Moas may have been strict herbivores, which is very rare among birds, or they may have supplemented their diet with insects, other invertebrates, and small vertebrates such as lizards.

Before humans arrived, the only predator capable of killing adult moas was the New Zealand Eagle (*Harpagornis*), the largest bird of prey known. Healthy adults of the larger moas may even have been too big for such a large predator. Moa eggs and chicks may have been eaten by smaller birds of prey, large rails, adzebills (*Aptornis*), skuas and gulls.

There were eleven species of moas, grouped into two families. Nine occurred in the South Island and seven in the North Island (see Table Three, page 181, for those restricted to one island). All the moa species, except the rare Crested Moa, have been found in archaeological sites. We can assume that all eleven moas were present when Polynesians reached New Zealand, and there is no proof that any European ever saw one. Moas therefore succumbed to the general ecological disruption, including direct hunting, that attended Maori settlement of New Zealand. The arrival of humans in New Zealand was so recent, and the occurrence of extinct birds in kitchen middens is, generally, so well documented, that the ultimate cause of the extinctions is obviously humans rather than late Pleistocene climatic change. There are old forest trees still living in the New Zealand bush that once sheltered or provided food for moas.

Many of the moas were already quite restricted in distribution when Maori arrived. The larger species may have been eliminated first. The Little Bush Moa, Large Bush Moa and the Upland Moa were possibly the last to die out, because the first two were so widely distributed and the last occurred in mountain habitats where humans rarely ventured. Archaeological evidence shows that moa hunting ceased as a major activity about 400 years ago. However, it may be that not all species were extinct by then.

The over-exploitation of moa populations may have begun at coastal sites chosen for their suitability for other purposes. When Maori hunted out the local moas, they may have established new settlements at other sites (including inland ones), where fresh moa populations could be exploited. In this way, successive changes in the pattern of settlement chased the moas into extinction.

Several factors additional to direct hunting probably contributed to the moas' demise. Maori burnt large areas of forest, especially in the eastern South Island, which destroyed some types of vegetative cover and encouraged others, presumably to the detriment of moas. The Kiore (*Rattus exulans*) — the south-east Asian rat introduced to New Zealand by Maori — probably killed moa chicks, and depleted the small animals and fallen berries that growing chicks may have relied on. As the rats colonised each new area their numbers would have reached plague proportions and had a very damaging effect before their population fell to a sustainable level. Maori domestic dogs may also have killed large numbers of moas. This would especially be so if the dogs ever established wild populations, though there is no evidence of this. If Maori ever brought chickens to New Zealand — again there is no evidence for this, though it is possible — they may have thus introduced avian diseases that affected moas.

Emeid Moas (Family Emeidae)

The emeid moas are: *Anomalopteryx* (one species), *Megalapteryx* (one species), *Pachyornis* (three species), *Emeus* (one species) and *Euryapteryx* (two species). They were generally less slender and less adapted for running than the dinornithid moas (Family Dinornithidae). *Pachyornis* and *Euryapteryx* were especially stoutly built, and had strong deep skulls and beaks.

Little Bush Moa

Anomalopteryx didiformis (Owen, 1844)
[Extinct]
A slender, lightly built species, estimated to have weighed about 30 kg. In a standing position it was probably about 1.3 m to the top of its head. It has been found in both main islands and on Stewart Island, and seems to have occurred mainly in lowland podocarp-broadleaf forest.

Upland Moa

Megalapteryx didinus (Owen, 1883)
[Extinct]
This small species was about the same size as the Little Bush Moa. Found only in the South Island, it occurred mainly in fairly open montane forest and subalpine herbfields and tussocklands up to at least 1800 m above sea level. It was common in the west and north-west but less so in the east. Mummified remains show that feathers extended on to the lower leg of the Upland Moa. This feature, and long toes, may have been adaptations for walking on soft snow. Greenish eggshell fragments are thought to be attributable to this species.

Heavy-footed Moa

Pachyornis elephantopus (Owen, 1856)
[Extinct]
This moa had short, massively thick leg bones, and was squat. It stood perhaps 1.8 m to the top of its head. It probably weighed about 145 kg, which is similar to the weight of an ostrich. The beak was pointed and the lower jaw very strong. The internal skull structure suggests that Heavy-footed Moas may have had a relatively acute sense of smell, like the kiwis. Found only in the South Island and on Stewart Island, this species was rare in dense bush, apparently preferring more open habitats in the east.

Crested Moa

Pachyornis australis Oliver, 1949
[Extinct]
The Crested Moa occurred only in the South Island where, unlike the Heavy-footed Moa, it favoured colder, wetter, western areas of montane and subalpine habitat. It was one of the smaller moas, weighing about 75 kg. Pits on the top of the skull, where large feathers may have been inserted, suggest that this species may have had a crest.

Mappin's Moa

Pachyornis mappini Archey, 1941
[Extinct]
This was a small species, not much more than a metre tall and probably weighing about 30 kg. It occurred only in the North Island, primarily in lowland areas. It was seemingly rare in dense forest, preferring scrub, forest edges and wetlands. The sexes differed in size, with females probably the larger, as in kiwis. This moa was named by G. Archey (later Sir Gilbert) after F.C. Mappin (later Sir Frank). They were companions on expeditions to search for moa bones in Waikaremoana and the King Country. Mappin found an almost complete skeleton of this species in a cave in 1933.

Eastern Moa

Emeus crassus (Owen, 1846)
[Extinct]

Found only in the South Island and possibly on Stewart Island, the Eastern Moa inhabited drier areas of scrub and low, open forest, and was very common in the east, especially in coastal areas. It was about 1.5 m tall and probably weighed about 70 kg. Analysis of several preserved gizzard contents has disclosed remains of fruits, seeds and leaves.

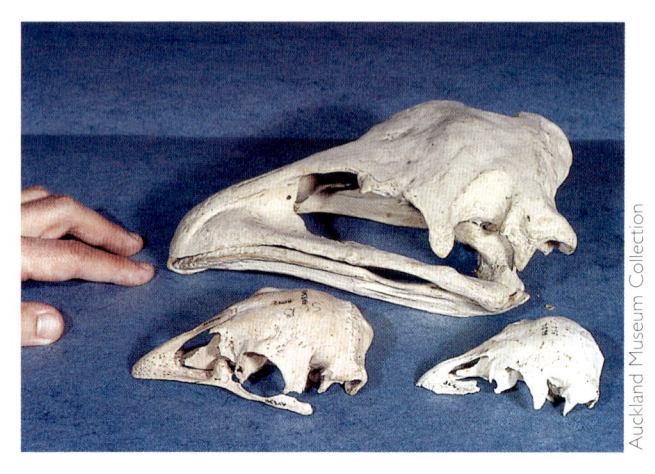

Moa skulls. Giant Moa (back, plaster cast), Eastern Moa (front left) and Coastal Moa.

Stout-legged Moa

Euryapteryx geranoides (Owen, 1848)
[Extinct]

The Stout-legged Moa was squat, with short legs and a broad pelvis. It grew to about 1.5 m tall and may have weighed about 90 kg. The bill was short and blunt and the jaw not particularly strong. This moa may have plucked foliage, rather than shearing it off, and eaten softer leaves than other species. Fossilised tracheal rings show that the windpipe in Stout-legged Moas was particularly bony, and so long (1.2 m) that it was looped. It may have acted as a resonating chamber, allowing this species to make loud trumpeting calls. Stout-legged Moas lived on all three main islands, preferring lowland areas of drier scrub and open forest. In the North Island they were apparently rare except in coastal areas from Hawke's Bay to Wairarapa. In the South Island they occurred mainly in the east, especially in dry, inland areas above 200 m.

Coastal Moa

Euryapteryx curtus (Owen, 1846)
[Extinct]

Found only in the North Island including Great Barrier Island, the Coastal Moa, like the Stout-legged and Eastern Moas, seems to have favoured drier, more open areas rather than dense wet forest. Its remains are very common in the dune sites of Northland. The sexes of the Coastal Moa differed in size, the female probably being the larger, as in kiwis. It was the smallest moa, about a metre tall to the top of its head, with a weight of about 20 kg. An egg of this species found at Doubtless Bay, Northland, around 1900, measures 120 mm by 91 mm, and is the smallest moa egg known. It has a capacity of just under 500 ml and at laying would have weighed nearly 500 g.

Above: Moa right femurs or thigh bones. Larger (back) from Giant Moa, smaller from Coastal Moa.

Below: Replicas of moa eggs. Smaller (left) believed to be from Coastal Moa, larger probably from Giant Moa.

Dinornithid Moas

(Family Dinornithidae)

The dinornithid moas were the three species of *Dinornis*. They had relatively longer lower leg bones (tarsometatarsi) than the emeid moas, and were generally taller, more slender and better adapted for running. The head was broad and flat, with a long, wide, down-curved beak. *Dinornis* means 'terrible bird', in the same way that dinosaurs were 'terrible lizards'.

Slender Bush Moa

Dinornis struthoides Owen, 1844
[Extinct]
The Slender Bush Moa was the smallest *Dinornis* — about 1.8 m tall with a weight of about 90 kg. It was found widely in the North and South Islands in forest from the lowlands to the subalpine zone. Its remains are less common in the South Island.

Large Bush Moa

Dinornis novaezealandiae Owen, 1843
[Extinct]
The Large Bush Moa was about 2.4 m tall, with an estimated weight of about 140 kg — intermediate in size between the other two species of *Dinornis* and about the same weight as an ostrich. It occurred throughout the North and South Islands in dense bush. It was the dominant dinornithid in wetter forests.

Giant Moa

Dinornis giganteus Owen, 1844
[Extinct]
Giant Moas occurred throughout the North Island and eastern South Island in lowland areas. They seem to have preferred scrub and low, open forest and to have shunned tall, dense bush. The Giant Moa was the tallest bird known; in an upright standing position it probably reached 3 m tall. The tallest living birds, the ostriches, stand about 2.5 m. However, the Giant Moa, estimated to have reached 270 kg, was not the heaviest bird. That title goes to *Aepyornis maximus*, one of the elephant birds of Madagascar, which probably weighed up to 460 kg. The largest moa egg yet found, excavated in the 1850s at Kaikoura, probably belonged to a Giant Moa. It is 240 mm by 178 mm with a capacity of nearly 4 litres — the equivalent of about 60 hens' eggs. When fresh it would have weighed nearly 4 kg.

Moa tracheal rings. Larger rings (left) from Giant Moa, smaller rings from Coastal Moa.

Kiwis

(Family Apterygidae)

This is the oldest surviving family of New Zealand birds. Kiwis are among the strangest of all living birds. They are the smallest of the ratites by a big margin, and also unusual among ratites in being nocturnal. Kiwis may have become nocturnal as a means of defence, given their small size. The other ratites, with longer legs, can more readily flee from predators, or defend themselves, and hence remain diurnal. The entire kiwi family of three species is endemic to New Zealand. It is sometimes put in an order of its own (the Apterygiformes). They are strangely shaped birds. The head is small and the body pear-shaped because the wings and flight muscles are undeveloped. The legs are relatively large and muscular, making up about a third of the total weight. When the Brown Kiwi was described in 1813, soon after the arrival in Britain of the first preserved specimen, it was thought by some to be a hoax.

The plumage of kiwis is hair-like and hangs loosely. There are no tail feathers, and the individual feathers — all of one type — lack an aftershaft (see Moas). The tiny vestigial wings are hidden in the body plumage, and end in a minute claw. There are bristle-like sensory feathers around the face. The nostrils open near the end of the long, down-curved bill, this condition being unique to kiwis. As they probe in the soil for prey, kiwis snuffle noisily as they forcefully exhale to clear their nasal passages. Unlike most birds, kiwis have a good sense of smell. They have four toes (as with moas), unlike other living ratites that have two or three toes.

Kiwis are so un-birdlike that they have been dubbed 'honorary mammals'. Their body temperature

Above: The immature Brown Kiwi has a shorter bill than the adult.

Right: A five-day-old Brown Kiwi chick leaving its nesting burrow at night.

Brown Kiwi.

and metabolic rate is slightly lower than for most birds and more like that of mammals. Males have a well-developed penis, as with other ratites but in contrast to most birds. Females have a pair of functional ovaries, whereas in most other birds the right ovary and oviduct are lost, which helps reduce weight for flight. If a kiwi lays more than one egg in a season, the ovaries function in turn, though all eggs pass through the left oviduct. Adults weigh 1.0–3.5 kg, depending on the species and sex. Females are larger and about 20 percent heavier than males.

Kiwis can live in forest and scrub from sea level to the subalpine zone. They eat seeds, berries, insects and other invertebrate animals that they find on or near the forest floor, or obtain by probing in soft earth and rotten logs. They nest in a hollow log, rock crevice or underground burrow which they excavate. The female produces one or two (very rarely three) eggs. The egg is very large — up to a quarter of the female's weight. It contains a high proportion of yolk, and after a long incubation (about 80 days) the resulting chick is very advanced — a miniature version of the adult. The chick has no egg-tooth and breaks out of the egg with its feet. Chicks are distended with stored yolk and unable to stand at first, but they leave the nest on foraging trips after about a week.

Brown Kiwi

Apteryx australis Shaw and Nodder, 1813

The Brown Kiwi has brown plumage with darker longitudinal streaks. It occurs on all three main islands but is now quite restricted in distribution. It is commonest in Northland and on Stewart Island. In some areas Brown Kiwis may survive in scrub, pine forests and rough farmland, especially where these abut native forest remnants or swamp. Some of the Northland populations have been decimated by rogue dogs. There is more hope for the future of Brown Kiwis on Stewart Island, which lacks stoats and where dogs are not a problem. The Brown Kiwi has traditionally been divided into North, South and Stewart Island subspecies. The North Island race is the smallest, while Stewart Island birds are the largest and have a peculiarity of emerging to forage on overcast days. Genetic studies have suggested that the Brown Kiwi is divisible not into three subspecies but into two separate species with the dividing line midway along the length of the South Island. This remains to be confirmed.

Above: A ten-day-old Brown Kiwi chick brooded under an adult male.

Little Spotted Kiwi

(Kiwi-Pukupuku)
Apteryx owenii Gould, 1847

This is the smallest and rarest of the kiwis. Both the Little Spotted Kiwi and Great Spotted Kiwi have greyish plumage with paler transverse streaks, giving a vaguely spotted appearance from a distance. The egg (300 g) relative to the size of the female (1325 g; 23 percent) is said to be larger than in any other species of bird (but see Grey Warbler). In pre-European times, Little Spotted Kiwis occurred throughout New Zealand but they are probably now extinct on the mainland. They survive on Kapiti Island near Wellington, and surplus stock has been transferred by the Department of Conservation to certain other predator-free offshore islands. This kiwi was named after Sir Richard Owen (1804–92) of the British Museum (Natural History) in London.

Above and left: Little Spotted Kiwi.

Great Spotted Kiwi.

Top: **Great Spotted Kiwi.**

Above: **Great Spotted Kiwi probing for food.**

Great Spotted Kiwi

(Roa)

Apteryx haastii Potts, 1872

This is the largest kiwi. As far as we know Great Spotted Kiwis were limited to the South Island and probably once lived throughout that island. This is hard to be certain of as their bones are difficult to separate from those of the Brown Kiwi. Today, Great Spotted Kiwis are found only in parts of the northern half of the South Island, in mixed podocarp forests west of the divide and in high-altitude beech forests to the east. Named in honour of Sir Julius von Haast (1822–87), one-time Director of the Canterbury Museum, Christchurch.

Fowl-like Birds
(Order GALLIFORMES)

The galliform or gallinaceous birds are cosmopolitan and include the guineafowls and New World quails as well as the members of the Phasianidae (see below). They are also called gamebirds because many species are hunted. Galliform birds are plump-bodied ground birds with short, strong legs and small heads. They have short, broad wings, and fly fast to escape danger, but the flight is low and not usually sustained. They lay large clutches, most commonly 6–15 eggs. In many species the downy young can fly within a few days of hatching. Seeds, roots, bulbs and other plant materials form the bulk of the diet in most species. A large crop accomodates gorging, and a powerful gizzard (with ingested grit) grinds tough and fibrous plant matter.

Grouse, Pheasants, Turkeys and Quails
(Family Phasianidae)

The family Phasianidae includes the pheasants, Old World quails, grouse and partridges, as well as domestic turkeys and chickens. They have powerful legs and are heavy birds that usually feed and nest on the ground, though they may roost in trees. They have short, rounded wings which allow them to fly quickly and strongly, but only for short distances. The feet are adapted for scratching. Most species eat vegetable foods — leaves, seeds, roots, berries — plus invertebrates to a variable degree. The unspecialised bill is short and thick.

New Zealand Quail.

New Zealand Quail

(Koreke)
Coturnix novaezelandiae Quoy and Gaimard, 1830
[Extinct]

This quail was encountered in the summer of 1769–70 on Cook's first voyage, but was not formally named until 1830 on the basis of a specimen collected on Auckland's North Shore. In the mid-1800s the New Zealand Quail may not have been very abundant in the North Island, but it was reportedly common throughout the South Island until about 1865 when it abruptly declined. The last known South Island specimens were taken in 1867 or 1868, and the last North Island sighting was at Taranaki in 1869. The New Zealand Quail was smaller than the introduced California Quail (*Callipepla californica*), and was said to be a weak flyer. It was a bird of open country; burning off to create pasture may have been a major factor in its extermination. It is also possible that the quail was reduced by a disease introduced along with the many species of gamebirds brought to New Zealand from the 1840s onwards. The New Zealand Quail has sometimes been considered a subspecies of the Stubble Quail (*Coturnix pectoralis*), which is widespread in Australia, but it now seems clear that they were distinct species.

Duck-like Birds

(Order ANSERIFORMES)

The anseriforms are web-footed, filter-feeding, swimming and diving birds (or derived from these). The eggs are unspotted and the hatchlings are clad in thick down. Research into bird relationships suggests that the anseriforms are closely related to the galliforms and that they branched from the other bird groups fairly early. There are three families of anseriforms: the screamers of South America, the Magpie Goose of Australia and New Guinea and the true wildfowl (Anatidae), which are cosmopolitan.

Swans, Geese and Ducks

(Family Anatidae)

The wildfowl or waterfowl are a large and successful group of aquatic birds with about 150 living species of which about twenty occur in New Zealand, some of them introduced. They are usually found on or close to water and have blunt, spoon-shaped bills with an elaborate filter-feeding mechanism unique to the anseriforms. Movement of the tongue draws water in at the end of the bill and expels it at the sides past filter plates (lamellae) which trap food particles. Species that have become grazers or fish-catchers still have vestiges of this system. The three forward-pointing toes are webbed and the plumage is thick and waterproof. Swans, geese and ducks usually nest on or near the ground, sometimes over water, and often near it. Nests are well-hidden and the downy young are led to water after hatching.

de Lautour's Duck

Biziura delautouri Forbes, 1892
[Extinct]

Subfossil bones of de Lautour's Duck have been found at a few North and South Island sites. It was named for Dr H. de Lautour of Oamaru, who helped the Canterbury Museum obtain moa bones from the area. Although it has been named as a distinct species, the New Zealand bird may prove to be identical to the living Musk Duck (*B. lobata*) of Australia, and more research is needed. New Zealand specimens may be slightly larger, but male Musk Ducks are much larger than females. This variation and a lack of specimens for comparison has frustrated a firm decision on the status of New Zealand birds. The Musk Duck is decidedly odd in appearance, the male having a large leathery flap hanging under its bill which features in the elaborate courtship display. The preen gland on the rump in males secretes a musky odour which intensifies during breeding.

New Zealand Swan

Cygnus sumnerensis (Forbes, 1892)
[Extinct]

There were no swans in New Zealand at the time of European settlement until Black Swans (*C. atratus*) were introduced from Australia (and perhaps arrived of their own accord) in the 1860s. Yet subfossil swan bones have been found throughout mainland New Zealand and on Stewart Island and the Chathams. The first bones were discovered by H.O. Forbes in 1890 in a cave at Sumner, Christchurch, and described as a new species. Bones have been found in Maori kitchen middens, proving the swan persisted after the arrival of humans. Bones of the New Zealand Swan were said to be larger and more robust than those of modern Black Swans. However, the two swans may be the same. If this is confirmed then the Black Swan was a New Zealand native bird that died out during Maori settlement, and the 'New Zealand Swan' did not exist.

North Island Goose

Cnemiornis gracilis Forbes, 1892
[Extinct]

The two species of New Zealand geese (*Cnemiornis*), both extinct, were larger relatives of the Cape Barren Goose (*Cereopsis novaehollandiae*) of Australia. Subfossil bones of the North Island Goose have been found throughout the North Island. It is also known as an early Pleistocene fossil (1–2 million years old) from Kai Iwi near Wanganui. This species was about three-quarters the size of the South Island Goose. Both had greatly reduced wing and pectoral bones, indicating that they were flightless. The bones of both have been found in archaeological middens proving that they became extinct after Maori settlement. They had broad beaks with a square end and were probably grazers living in more open areas — wetlands, scrub, grassland and the edges of rivers and forest.

South Island Goose

Cnemiornis calcitrans Owen, 1865
[Extinct]

The first bones of a giant New Zealand goose were found in a limestone crevice near Timaru about 1863. Remains of the South Island Goose have now been found in caves and swamps in the eastern half of the South Island from Marlborough to Southland, and in the north-west. It stood about 1 m tall and may have weighed 10–15 kg, which is very large for a goose.

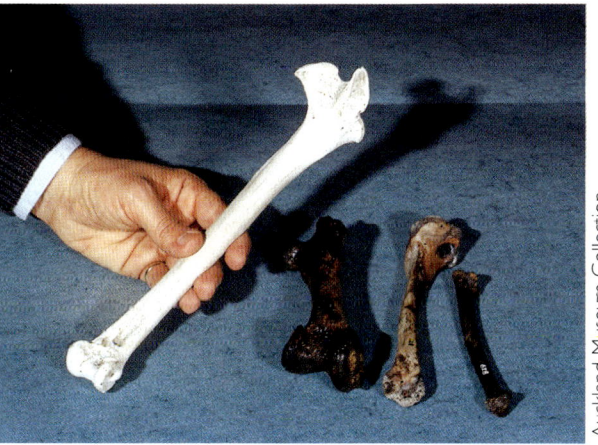

Bones of South Island Goose.

Finsch's Duck

Euryanas finschi (Van Beneden, 1875)
[Extinct]

This duck is so distinctive anatomically that it is placed in a subfamily of its own (the Euryanatinae) which is a sister-group to the shelducks and typical ducks. The first bones of this duck were found in a cave at Earnscleugh, Central Otago, that had been discovered by a boy in about 1870. The bones were sent to Dr Otto Finsch (1839–1917) in Germany, who passed them to Professor Van Beneden. The description of the new duck was published in 1875 and Van Beneden named it after Finsch. Subfossil bones of Finsch's Duck have been found widely in the North and South Islands, especially in caves, and they occur in Maori kitchen middens. It was a heavily built duck, perhaps weighing a little over 2 kg. Research has suggested that it was a strong flier more than 10,000 years ago, and then steadily lost its flying capacity until it could no longer engage in sustained flight. It seems that Finsch's Duck was a strong-walking, terrestrial duck with stout legs and a short bill, inhabiting grassland, open scrub and forest edges and remaining fairly independent of open water.

Female Paradise Shelduck.

Paradise Shelduck

(Putangitangi)
Tadorna variegata (Gmelin, 1789)

A local representative of a distinct subfamily of large, goose-like ducks, many of which are semi-terrestrial. Paradise Shelducks are the largest duck in New Zealand, leaving aside the Australian representative of the group — the Chestnut-breasted Shelduck, *T. tadornoides* — which is seen occasionally in New Zealand and is known to have bred here a couple of times. The sexes differ strikingly; male Paradise Shelducks have a black head (with a glossy green tinge) and a dark body; females have a white head and an orange-brown body. They are often seen in pairs and occur throughout New Zealand in farmland and other open areas, especially where there are ponds and lakes. They are persistently noisy with loud alarm calls, often given while circling in flight. The male and female call in turn, the male giving a deep honk and the female a shriller call. Paradise Shelducks gather in large flocks to moult in summer (December–February). An increase in pasture and farm dams has made them more numerous and widespread now than late last century, despite legal hunting.

Duck-like Birds 39

Left: Paradise Shelducks in flight.

Below: A pair of Paradise Shelducks with five-day-old ducklings.

Male Paradise Shelduck.

Blue Ducks inhabit fast-flowing streams in forested high country.

Blue Duck

(Whio)
Hymenolaimus malacorhynchos (Gmelin, 1789)

This is the strangest of New Zealand's living ducks because of its bill, which is adapted for feeding in mountain streams. It prefers fast-flowing water, so is mainly found in or near turbulent montane rivers and streams in the forested high country of both main islands. The blue-grey plumage is excellent camouflage among boulders. Blue Ducks feed almost exclusively on aquatic insects, especially caddis-fly larvae, obtained from among rocks and stones in shallow white water. In deeper water they dive for food. Adults have a soft, black flap on each side at the end of the bill. These are thought to protect the bill as it rubs against rocks. The ducklings have large feet which help them to swim against the current. Adult males give a whistling call that is high-pitched and wheezy, and can be heard above the roar of flowing water; the basis of the Maori name. Pairs keep territories all year. Except for family groups, Blue Ducks are not gregarious.

Duck-like Birds 41

Top and above: Blue Duck pairs.

Right: A Blue Duck pair with seven three-week-old ducklings.

Left: Brown Teal prefer rivers and streams where dense vegetation covers the banks.

Below: A pair of Brown Teal.

Brown Teal

(Pateke)
Anas chlorotis G.R. Gray, 1845

The Brown Teal is New Zealand's endemic representative of the cosmopolitan genus *Anas*, the typical ducks. It probably shares a common ancestor with Australia's Chestnut Teal (*A. castanea*) which it resembles closely in colouring. Brown Teal have declined since the nineteenth century, when they were widespread in lowland swamp and swamp forests. With a total population of less than 2500, they are vulnerable to extinction. Today their stronghold is Great Barrier Island, and parts of Northland. They frequent heavily vegetated wetlands, especially lagoons and tidal reaches of streams, and prefer areas with some slow-flowing or still, open water. When disturbed they are reluctant to fly. They are occasionally seen in Fiordland but are now extinct on Stewart Island. It is possible that before the advent of mammalian predators they were more terrestrial, foraging on the forest floor and ascending forested ridges. They are gregarious and form large flocks outside the breeding season. They often feed at night.

Auckland Island Teal

Anas aucklandica (G.R. Gray, 1844)
[Outlying islands only]

This is one of the very few flightless ducks. The wings are noticeably reduced, but they are flapped when the ducks 'skitter' over the water, and are used to assist in scrambling over rocks. Auckland Island Teal are found only at the subantarctic Auckland group where they have gone from the main Auckland Island, but persist on half a dozen smaller inshore islands. This and the Campbell Island Teal are often considered to be subspecies of the Brown Teal of mainland New Zealand, but evidence is mounting that they are distinct species. Auckland Island Teal are smaller and darker than Brown Teal. They are mainly nocturnal and feed in streams and on the shore-

Duck-like Birds

The flightless Auckland Island Teal (captive).

ducks with a population not above 100 birds. When disturbed they run rapidly with their necks stretched forward and their bodies hunched.

Chatham Island Duck

Pachyanas chathamica Oliver, 1955
[Extinct. Outlying islands only]

The Chatham Island Duck was described from subfossil bones found at the Chatham Islands. It had a very robust skull and was stoutly built, perhaps weighing 2 kg — twice as much as a Grey Duck (*Anas superciliosa*). The Chatham Island Duck was probably incapable of powered flight. It may have been marine, feeding on crabs and shellfish caught close to the shore. Bones have been found in Moriori kitchen middens.

Scarlett's Duck

Malacorhynchus scarletti Olson, 1977
[Extinct]

During excavations of the Pyramid Valley swamp in North Canterbury, beginning in 1939, some bones of a new duck were found. These bones, belonging to at least four individuals, are about 3500 years old. They are now recognised as belonging to a bird similar to the Pink-eared Duck (*M. membranaceus*) of Australia, but much larger. In addition, one bone of this species has been found in Marlborough and one in Hawke's Bay. In Australia, Pink-eared Ducks prefer shallow, open water, and Scarlett's Duck may have been largely restricted to open areas and swamps where it could dabble in shallow water. The bill of the Pink-eared Duck has a large, square end with small flaps — a specialisation for filter-feeding. The bill of Scarlett's Duck was similar, and the diet was therefore probably small crustaceans and insects. The duck was named after Ron Scarlett (1911–), osteologist at Canterbury Museum, Christchurch.

line, often foraging among piles of rotting seaweed cast ashore. They also feed among kelp growing in sheltered bays. The ducks occur all over some of the islands, in areas of tussock and in rata (*Metrosideros*) forest. The current population exceeds 2000 birds. Pairs have territories in which they remain all year, but young and unpaired birds may flock together in sheltered bays.

Campbell Island Teal

Anas nesiotis (Fleming, 1935)
[Outlying islands only]

This species is flightless like the Auckland Island Teal, and has short, feeble wings. It is even smaller than its Auckland Island relative. It disappeared from the main Campbell Island after the introduction of cats and rats, and was thought likely to be extinct, until 1975 when a population was discovered on tiny Dent Island, off-lying Campbell Island. It is one of the world's rarest

New Zealand Scaup

(Papango)

Aythya novaeseelandiae (Gmelin, 1789)

This is New Zealand's only endemic diving duck. As with many other endemic species this duck has declined since the 1800s. It is widely distributed, but uncommon in most areas, preferring large, open lakes with deep, clear water. In the North Island, New Zealand Scaups have adapted well to hydroelectric dams. They dive several metres under water to pluck aquatic plants, snails and insects from the bottom. Propulsion during the dive comes from the feet not the wings. The New Zealand Scaup may be a close relative of the Hardhead, *A. australis*, of Australia, but it has been suggested that the two species had independent origins from Northern Hemisphere ancestors.

Auckland Island Merganser

Mergus australis Hombron and Jacquinot, 1841
[Extinct]

Mergansers, also called sea ducks because many frequent inshore waters, are ducks with long, thin bills. Both parts of the beak (maxilla and mandible) are armed with backward-facing serrations, adapted for seizing and holding fish. Apart from a species in Brazil, and the Auckland Island Merganser, they are restricted to the Northern Hemisphere. In historical times the Auckland Island Merganser was recorded only at two islands in the subantarctic Auckland group (600 km south-west of Invercargill), namely, Auckland Island itself and the adjacent Adams Island. The first specimen was collected in March 1840 by Lieutenant Jacquinot of the French ship *Astrolabe*. The last specimens to be seen were probably the pair shot on 9 January 1902 by Mr Shattock, a member of the staff of the Governor

Above left: New Zealand Scaup with ducklings.

Left: A female New Zealand Scaup.

Duck-like Birds 45

New Zealand Scaup.

of New Zealand. However, subfossil bones from both natural deposits and Maori kitchen middens have been found widely in North, South, Stewart and the Chatham Islands, suggesting that the Polynesian occupation of New Zealand caused the extinction of this species at temperate latitudes. The population at the Auckland Islands was clearly a remnant at the edge of the species' range, and the collecting of museum specimens may have been a significant factor in its demise. The Auckland Island Merganser was the smallest of all mergansers, weighing about 900 g, but it possessed the longest bill. The wings were reduced but this merganser apparently could still fly. Uniquely among mergansers the sexes were alike in plumage, and adults bore a crest on their heads.

A male New Zealand Scaup.

Grebes

(Order PODICIPEDIFORMES, Family Podicipedidae)

Grebes are freshwater, foot-propelled, diving birds with lobed feet and thick, waterproof plumage. The strong feet, which sit well towards the rear as the birds float, enable grebes to swim strongly at the surface and to dive under water for food and to escape danger. Their legs function poorly on land and grebes rarely come ashore. Nests are usually a floating mass of sodden vegetation, often in shallow water or tethered to plants at the water's edge. Chicks often travel about on the back of the swimming adult.

New Zealand Dabchick.

New Zealand Dabchick

(Weweia)

Poliocephalus rufopectus (G.R. Gray, 1843)

Now restricted to the North Island, the New Zealand Dabchick was present in low numbers in the South Island during the nineteenth century, but died out for reasons unknown. The population is thought to be less than 2000 but the birds are widespread on farm dams, sewage oxidation ponds, coastal lagoons and larger inland lakes with shallow, sheltered edges. When disturbed, Dabchicks swim away (on or beneath the surface) or skitter across the water with beating wings striking the surface. They can swim faster under water than on the surface. Dabchicks do not fly except at night, and they are silent. They eat aquatic insects, water snails, freshwater crayfish and fish.

Top left: New Zealand Dabchick. Chicks are fed by both parents who also take turns to carry them.

Above left: New Zealand Dabchick. A chick reveals its lobe-webbed foot.

Top right: New Zealand Dabchick with eggs.

Above right: New Zealand Dabchicks copulating.

Penguins

(Order SPHENISCIFORMES, Family Spheniscidae)

Penguins are flightless seabirds found only in the Southern Hemisphere. They are descended from flying birds and their wings are modified into short, stiff flippers which make them excellent swimmers. Essentially they fly under water, propelled by the flippers alone. Penguins have short legs and walk with a waddling gait. The three forward-pointing toes are webbed. The feathers are short and densely packed, forming a smooth, firm, water-resistant exterior. During the moult, penguins lose their waterproofing and must stay ashore, fasting for several weeks. All modern penguins are similar in shape, despite their range of sizes (1–30 kg) and their variation in habitat; they breed on ice, beaches, bare lava, and in tussock grassland and temperate forest. Penguins are characteristic of the New Zealand region, and New Zealand has an important fossil record of the penguins.

Below left: After preening itself the penguin then makes its way to its nest.

Below right: A Yellow-eyed Penguin leaves the surf.

Yellow-eyed Penguin

(Hoiho)

Megadyptes antipodes (Hombron and Jacquinot, 1841)
Distinctive enough to warrant a genus of its own, this is one of the world's rarest penguins, and the largest of the three penguins that breed on the New Zealand mainland. Yellow-eyed Penguins breed in the south-east of the South Island, from Banks Peninsula to Stewart Island, and on the subantarctic Auckland and Campbell Islands. They are fairly sedentary, so the distribution is much the same in winter as during the breeding season, though stragglers — especially juveniles — may fetch up in other parts of New Zealand. Pairs nest in or around low, scrubby vegetation, spaced apart and out of sight of their neighbours. One tagged wild bird has lived over 30 years. Yellow-eyed Penguins eat fish, cephalopods and crustaceans, which they get by diving as deep as 160 m below the surface.

Above left: Late in the day another penguin comes back to its nest.

Above right: A Yellow-eyed Penguin at the nest with a well-grown chick.

Fiordland Crested Penguin

(Pokotiwha)

Eudyptes pachyrhynchus G.R. Gray, 1845

This penguin belongs to a group of species, the crested penguins, that inhabit the subantarctic islands south of Australia and New Zealand. The Fiordland Crested Penguin is slightly smaller than the Yellow-eyed Penguin. It breeds only in New Zealand, in coastal forest and on the remote rocky shore of south Westland, Fiordland, the Foveaux Strait area and Stewart Island. Fiordland Crested Penguins nest in caves, rocky crevices or among tree roots, singly or in small colonies of up to ten pairs. This is unlike the other crested penguins, which nest in large colonies in the open. After the chicks fledge, adult Fiordland Crested Penguins go to sea for a couple of months, then return to the breeding site to moult. As with the other New Zealand penguins, they remain ashore fasting during the moult and cannot swim once they lose their waterproofing feathers. Birds may straggle to other parts of New Zealand and some vagrants have reached southern Australia. Bones from subfossil deposits and Maori middens show that this penguin once occurred more widely in both South and North Islands.

Above left: Fiordland Crested Penguins on rocks at Open Bay Island, Fiordland.

Left: Fiordland Crested Penguin moulting, Open Bay Island.

Left: Pair of Fiordland Crested Penguins at their nest, Jackson Head.

Snares Crested Penguin

Eudyptes robustus Oliver, 1953
[Outlying islands only]
This species is similar to the Fiordland Crested Penguin but slightly larger. It breeds only on the Snares Islands. The breeding colonies are dense, usually on bare ground under low forest or among tussocks. Each female lays two eggs in a shallow nest, but rarely more than one chick survives. At twenty days old the chicks leave the nest and join others in a crèche where they are fed by their own parents. While breeding, adults forage in waters close to the Snares and they moult at the nesting colonies before dispersing in winter. Stragglers, especially moulting immatures, are occasionally found on Stewart Island and South Island beaches, and even more distant localities such as the Chatham Islands and southern Australia. Snares Crested Penguins eat krill, squids and small fish.

Erect-crested Penguin

Eudyptes sclateri Buller, 1888
[Outlying islands only]
This subantarctic penguin breeds in large numbers on the Antipodes and Bounty Islands, with a handful breeding on Disappointment Island in the Auckland group. Its pattern of movement associated with breeding and moulting is similar to that of the Snares Crested Penguin, with stragglers reaching the New Zealand mainland and Australia. Named for P.L. Sclater (1829–1913), a British zoologist.

Tube-nosed Seabirds

(Order PROCELLARIIFORMES)

The tube-nosed seabirds are second only to the penguins in their advanced adaptations to life at sea. The surface of the hooked bill comprises various horny plates separated by grooves. The external nostrils are enclosed in a tube, and the sense of smell is well developed. The wings are long and pointed as befits strong-flying birds that must cover long distances at sea in search of food. Many species soar and glide extensively to exploit strong winds and conserve effort. The three forward-pointing toes are webbed. Many species come ashore voluntarily only to breed and most are clumsy on land. New Zealand has a magnificent diversity of procellariiform seabirds. At sea they may be seen in spectacular feeding, roosting or migrating flocks of tens of thousands of individuals. However, because they feed at sea and nest on inaccessible islands or headlands, they are rarely seen from land, and their importance and numbers go unnoticed. Their bodies wash up on beaches, especially after storms, and the identification and counting of these corpses is a major project of the Ornithological Society of New Zealand.

Shearwaters, Fulmars, Prions and Petrels

(Family Procellariidae)

The Procellariidae is the largest family of tube-nosed birds. Of the 70-odd species in the world, nearly 50 have been recorded in the New Zealand region. They range in size from the giant petrels, which are heavier than a mollymawk, to the diminutive diving petrels. Most species of Procellariidae nest in colonies and the individual nests are usually in burrows or crevices. Adults usually return to the colony at night to avoid attack from daytime predators like hawks and skuas. At the start of the breeding season pairs clean out the burrow and bring dried plant material to form a nest. The birds of a pair copulate and then go to sea for several weeks (the 'pre-laying exodus'). The female returns to lay one white egg. The sexes take turns to incubate and the incubation period is long, often six to eight weeks. The

Tube-nosed Seabirds

Buller's Shearwaters.

chick is guarded for the first few days, then left for several days between feeds while the parents forage at sea. The chick grows rapidly and greatly exceeds the adult weight. Towards the end of the long nestling period (two to five months), the parents abandon the chick and it loses weight before its first flight. Most species do not breed until they are several years old, so once the chick has flown from the breeding colony it is unlikely to set foot on land again for several years.

Petrels and their allies are awkward on the ground and often cannot take to the air easily if disturbed. This, and the fact that nestlings are left unattended for long periods, means that both adults and young are particularly vulnerable to predation. In the New Zealand area these seabirds nest on islands that are free of introduced mammalian predators. However, the record of fossil bones shows that until recently many were widespread on the main islands. Colonies that must have once existed on ridges throughout New Zealand have now largely been eliminated by predators.

Buller's Shearwater

Puffinus bulleri Salvin, 1888

In common with all shearwaters, this handsome seabird has a long, narrow bill that is hooked at the end — well adapted for seizing prey at the surface of the sea. This is a large shearwater and it undertakes a spectacular annual migration between New Zealand and the North Pacific. It has a total population estimated at about 2.5 million birds, and they breed only on seven of the twelve islands of the Poor Knights group east of Whangarei. However, they probably once bred more widely since subfossil bones have been found on both main islands of New Zealand and on the Chatham Islands. Buller's Shearwaters are colonial nesters, each pair producing one white egg in their burrow on the forest floor. Most eggs are laid in November and most chicks develop in time to leave the colony in May. Adults are widespread in New Zealand waters, but especially in the north (Northland, Hauraki Gulf, Bay of Plenty, East Cape), between early September and the middle of May. A few birds are also found in eastern Australian waters at this time. In late autumn (April–May) Buller's Shearwaters migrate to the North Pacific, fetching up in an arc from Japan to the west coast of North America. Most of them probably move within this arc from west to east, then they move south, returning to New Zealand in late August and early September. This species was named after Sir Walter Buller (1838–1906), the famous New Zealand naturalist.

Above left: Buller's Shearwater showing distinctive upper wing markings.

Left: Buller's Shearwaters.

Tube-nosed Seabirds 55

Fluttering Shearwaters.

Fluttering Shearwater.

Fluttering Shearwater

(Pakaha)
Puffinus gavia (Forster, 1844)

This is one of the smaller shearwaters and it inhabits coastal waters rather than the open ocean. They breed on islands along the north-east coast between the Three Kings Islands and Gisborne, and in the Marlborough Sounds area. They are thus very common seabirds in the Hauraki Gulf, the Bay of Plenty and in Cook Strait. Fluttering Shearwaters remain close to their breeding islands in spring and summer but in autumn and winter they range more widely over the waters of the New Zealand continental shelf. At the end of the breeding season, many fledglings migrate to the coastal waters of south-east Australia. Fluttering Shearwaters will dive as deep as ten metres in pursuit of prey, using their feet and wings for propulsion.

Hutton's Shearwater

Puffinus huttoni Mathews, 1912

Hutton's Shearwater is superficially very similar to the Fluttering Shearwater apart from less white and more brownish-grey on the underwings. It breeds only in the seaward Kaikoura Range on the north-east coast of the South Island. Hutton's Shearwaters used to breed in the neighbouring inland Kaikoura Range, and they probably bred elsewhere in the eastern South Island. In the breeding season (spring and summer), Hutton's Shearwaters are seen in coastal waters east of the South Island and in the Cook Strait area. In autumn many migrate to Australian waters, as far north as Torres Strait and the north-west coast of Western Australia. It is not known whether individuals fly around the continent in the course of their migration or take the same path there and back. They return to New Zealand between August and November. Though the species was described and named in 1912, the breeding sites — tussock- and scrub-covered slopes at 1200–1800 m — were not discovered until 1965. In colder years breeding may be delayed by a week or two if late snow prevents adults from entering their burrows. This bird is named after F.W. Hutton (1836–1905), a prominent New Zealand zoologist.

Scarlett's Shearwater

Puffinus spelaeus Holdaway and Worthy, 1994
[Extinct]

This species was described on the basis of abundant fossil bones from caves in the west and north-west of the South Island. The bones suggest that the shearwater was breeding in the vicinity of the caves, presumably in colonies on forested ridges nearby. The bones range in age from at least 20,000 years old to less than 600 years old, making this a species that must have succumbed to ecological disruption during Maori settlement, most likely from the deleterious effect of the Kiore (*Rattus exulans*). Scarlett's Shearwater was closely related to the Fluttering and Hutton's Shearwaters but was slightly smaller than both. The breeding ranges of the three species probably did not overlap. The common name, Scarlett's Shearwater, reflects the fact that Ron Scarlett (see Scarlett's Duck) recognised this species many years ago.

Black Petrel

Procellaria parkinsoni G.R. Gray, 1862

The *Procellaria* petrels are big, heavily built seabirds that feed well out at sea, making them seldom seen near land. They are the largest of the burrow-nesting seabirds. Today Black Petrels breed only in the hills of Little and Great Barrier Islands but they once bred in the coastal ranges of the North Island and the north-west corner of the South Island. The burrows are excavated on ridgetops in soil or peat, often among tree roots. Black Petrel chicks were the largest kind of muttonbirds available to North Island Maori, and were harvested on the mainland until the early days of European settlement. The success of the small Little Barrier colony was improved with

Westland Petrel outside breeding burrow, Punakaiki, West Coast.

Tube-nosed Seabirds

Westland Petrel.

Below: Black Petrel.

the eradication of feral cats on that island in 1980. The total population now numbers 3000–4000 birds. In spring and summer Black Petrels are found in the waters around northern New Zealand and some reach south-eastern Australia. Even while breeding they may move hundreds of kilometres in search of food, which is mainly bioluminescent squid caught at night. Between March and July they migrate to the eastern tropical Pacific from southern Mexico to northern Peru and near the Galapagos Islands. Breeding birds return to New Zealand between October and December. Named in honour of Sydney Parkinson (1745–71), artist on Cook's first voyage, who died on the return journey.

Westland Petrel

Procellaria westlandica Falla, 1946

The Westland Petrel is similar in appearance to the Black Petrel but slightly larger. It nests in the dense, lowland forest of the foothills of the Paparoa Range, Westland. It has an unusual winter breeding season, which is very long. The colonies are reoccupied in February–March, most eggs are laid in May and chicks fledge in November–December. During the breeding season, birds forage in the waters of the continental shelf east and west of central New Zealand. In summer they disperse more widely, reaching south-east Australia and the coast of South America. This species has been increasing. Westland Petrels are strong and fierce enough to repel mammalian predators, and fish scraps discarded by commercial fishing vessels have provided a steady source of food close to the breeding colonies.

Above: A pair of Pycroft's Petrels near their nest burrow.

Above right: A Pycroft's Petrel in an elevated tree fork prior to take-off.

Pycroft's Petrel

Pterodroma pycrofti Falla, 1933

Members of the genus *Pterodroma* belong to a group known as the 'gadfly petrels'. They are medium-sized to large seabirds, oceanic in their preferences and rarely seen near land. Pycroft's Petrel is one of the smaller gadfly petrels. It breeds on islands off the north-eastern coast of the North Island, especially certain islands of the Poor Knights, Hen and Chickens and Mercury groups. Although now endemic to New Zealand, subfossil bones show that the species once bred on Norfolk and Lord Howe Islands. During the breeding season (October–April), Pycroft's Petrels may be seen at sea in waters east of the northern half of the North Island. For the rest of the year they are believed to migrate to the North Pacific, but details are uncertain. On Aorangi in the Poor Knights group, Pycroft's Petrels are sometimes forced to share their burrows with tuataras, and occasional adults and chicks probably fall prey to these reptiles. Named in honour of A.T. Pycroft (1875–1971), an amateur naturalist from Auckland.

Tube-nosed Seabirds

Above: Cook's Petrel.

Above right: Cook's Petrel preening.

Cook's Petrel

(Titi)
Pterodroma cookii (G.R. Gray, 1843)

This species is almost identical in appearance to Pycroft's Petrel, but is a little larger, with a slightly longer bill. The two species cannot be distinguished at sea. Cook's Petrels once bred at suitable sites throughout New Zealand, but today they breed on the forested ridges of only three islands; Little Barrier and Great Barrier in the north, and Codfish in the south. The breeding season is roughly the same as for Pycroft's Petrel, though preparation of the burrows by Cook's Petrels may begin as early as late-August in the north. During the New Zealand summer Cook's Petrels range at sea, mainly east of their breeding islands. After the breeding season they migrate to the eastern Pacific between Chile and Mexico with stragglers reaching the Gulf of Alaska. Named for Captain James Cook (1718–79), the English navigator.

Mottled Petrel

(Korure)
Pterodroma inexpectata (Forster, 1844)

One of the medium-sized gadfly petrels, this species gets its name from the grey mottling on its white face. Mottled Petrels nest in southern New Zealand on islands in Fiordland, on some of Stewart Island's offliers and at The Snares. They used to breed on the North, South and Chatham Islands. In the breeding season (late October to June) they range widely in the seas around southern New Zealand, through subantarctic waters to the pack-ice and occasionally to south-east Australia. After the breeding season, Mottled Petrels migrate to subarctic waters in the North Pacific and Bering Sea.

Chatham Petrel

Pterodroma axillaris (Salvin, 1893)
[Outlying islands only]

The Chatham Petrel is one of the world's rarest petrels, with a total population of less than 1000. It now breeds only on South East Island in the Chatham group. However, Holocene fossil bones show that it once bred on other islands in the group, but these colonies died out after Moriori settlement. Chatham Petrels were rediscovered on South East Island in 1973, after an absence of records for 30 years. Adults return to the island in late November and early December to prepare their burrows and court. The nests are spread among those of other petrels. The single egg hatches between February and April and the chick fledges between May and July. Because it is so rare its range at sea is unknown, but it probably migrates to the North Pacific between June and November.

Magenta Petrel

Pterodroma magentae (Giglioli and Salvadori, 1869)
[Outlying islands only]

Magenta Petrels, also called Chatham Island Taikos, are one of the world's rarest birds, with a total population believed to be less than 100. They were thought extinct until 1973, when four birds were attracted to bright lights, and two were caught five years later. Measurements and photographs of the live birds confirmed that they were the same as the Magenta Petrel described in 1869. This bird is named Magenta after the Italian warship of this name, aboard which the first specimen was taken in the central South Pacific in the winter of 1867. It was once abundant on the Chatham Islands, as evidenced by the presence of fossil bones in natural sites and Moriori middens, but now breeds only on forested ridges of the south-west of Chatham Island. After breeding, Magenta Petrels are assumed to migrate to the central South Pacific.

Albatrosses and Mollymawks
(Family Diomedeidae)

The albatrosses are the largest of the tube-nosed seabirds. 'Mollymawk' is used in New Zealand for the smaller albatrosses. Albatrosses have long, narrow wings which they hold out stiffly. They travel vast trans-oceanic distances, exploiting updraughts over the waves to achieve graceful, effortless, gliding flight. If the wind drops they settle on the water. They come ashore only to breed and are awkward on land. The long, heavy bill is hooked for seizing slippery prey. Albatrosses do not construct burrows but lay their egg in an open, shallow nest of compacted vegetation and mud. The extremely long breeding cycle lasts seven to eleven months from courtship to fledging of the chick. The albatrosses, as with the tube-noses in general, reach their greatest diversity and numbers in the Southern Hemisphere. Ten of the fourteen species of albatrosses have been recorded in the New Zealand region.

Royal Albatross in flight.

Tube-nosed Seabirds 61

Top left: A pair of immature Royal Albatrosses indulging in mild courtship behaviour.

Top right: A Royal Albatross at its nest on the Taiaroa Heads sanctuary.

Above: A Royal Albatross incubating its single egg.

Royal Albatross

(Toroa)

Diomedea epomophora Lesson, 1825

This is the largest of all the procellariiform seabirds (though the Wandering Albatross, *D. exulans*, is more or less as big), with a weight of about 9 kg. The wingspan of these two species — up to 3.5 m — is the largest of any bird. Royal Albatrosses nest in loose colonies on the Auckland, Campbell and Chatham Islands and at Taiaroa Head at the entrance to Otago Harbour, near Dunedin. Taiaroa Head is the only place in the world where albatrosses nest on the mainland. Eggs are laid from late October to mid-December. The incubation period of this species (and the Wandering Albatross) can exceed 80 days, which is the longest of any bird. Chicks are not ready to fledge until August to December of the following year. Adults that successfully raise a chick wait a year before breeding again. Royal Albatrosses normally do not begin to breed until six to ten years old. The oldest of all the wild birds banded in New Zealand was a Royal Albatross (nicknamed 'Grandma') that lived at least 52 years, probably 60. Royal Albatrosses may be seen throughout coastal New Zealand waters and in the Tasman Sea, at all times, but especially in winter. They disperse throughout sub-antarctic seas. Many non-breeders, and birds too young to breed, migrate east to waters off South America. They return to New Zealand via the southern Indian Ocean and the seas south of Australia.

Buller's Mollymawk

Thalassarche bulleri Rothschild, 1893

This species has two subspecies which differ slightly in their bill-size and head plumage, but differ greatly in their breeding season. The nominate race (*Th. bulleri bulleri*) breeds on The Snares and the Solander Islands from January to October. The other subspecies (*Th. bulleri platei*) breeds at the Chatham Islands and on Rosemary Rocks of the Three Kings group from October to June. Buller's Mollymawks are often seen in coastal waters around southern New Zealand. They range across the Tasman Sea to south-east Australian waters, and an unknown proportion of the population migrates anually to the coasts of Chile and Peru. They mostly pair for life, as is typical of albatrosses. One pair, banded in 1948, was still returning to use the same nest 23 years later, and when last seen the female was at least 50 years old. Named after Buller (see Buller's Shearwater).

Above: A Buller's Mollymawk.

Left: Buller's Mollymawks near Stewart Island.

Pelicans, Gannets, Cormorants and Allies

(Order PELECANIFORMES)

The pelecaniforms are medium-sized to large water-birds that mostly eat fish. They have totipalmate feet — their four toes are connected by three webs. The upper part of the bill is composed of several plates. A pair of salt glands near the nostrils eliminates excess dietary salt. Most pelecaniform birds have a bare-skinned, distensible throat (gular) pouch with several functions. It can help to enclose prey before swallowing (developed to an extreme in pelicans), or may have a visual role in displays. To lose heat, pelecaniform birds gape and flutter their throat pouch, exposing their moist throat lining to evaporative cooling. Undigested food-remains are regurgitated and only fluids pass from the stomach to the intestine. The webbed feet are used to help incubate eggs. In all except the tropic birds, the eggs are pale with a chalky coating. There are six families — pelicans, gannets and boobies, darters, cormorants and shags, frigatebirds and tropicbirds. New Zealand has endemic species in two of these families.

Cormorants and Shags
(Family Phalacrocoracidae)

Twelve members of this family breed in the New Zealand area, about a third of the world's species. In New Zealand the term 'shag' is applied to all, a name which originates from the tuft-like crests on the head, mainly evident during breeding. Elsewhere, 'cormorant' is used for the species of *Phalacrocorax*, which are mainly freshwater birds. Shags in general are long-necked waterbirds with long, strongly hooked beaks used to catch fish and crustaceans pursued by diving. They swim low in the water, the reduction in buoyancy achieved by modifications of the body feathers (which allow air to escape the plumage and water to enter), and (in some species) by the ingesting of pebbles. When ashore, shags shake water out of the plumage, and the species of *Phalacrocorax* (but not *Leucocarbo* and *Stictocarbo*) perch in a characteristic way with their wings spread out to dry. *Phalacrocorax* shags have black feet and can perch on branches and wires, while *Leucocarbo* and *Stictocarbo* shags have pink or yellow feet (respectively) and cannot perch on thin supports. Shags typically breed in colonies.

Above: A colony of King Shags.

Above right: King Shags.

King Shag

Leucocarbo carunculatus (Gmelin, 1789)

This large shag is one of the world's rarest, with a total population of about 500. Today it is found only in the coastal waters of the Marlborough Sounds, but subfossil bones from northern parts of the South Island, and from Northland, show that the distribution was once wider. They nest colonially on a handful of exposed rocks, reefs and islets, and they feed in sheltered marine inlets and bays. King Shags feed on bottom-dwelling fish and crustaceans. The latinised name *carunculatus* refers to fleshy yellow-orange swellings called caruncles at the base of the upper part of the bill. During breeding, bare skin on the face and throat changes colour from a grey-blue to reddish.

Stewart Island Shag

Leucocarbo chalconotus (G.R. Gray, 1845)

The Stewart Island Shag occurs in two colour forms. The pied form is similar to the King Shag, but the 'bronze' form is brownish black with a metallic sheen. The two forms freely interbreed, producing offspring of one form or the other, but rare intermediates are also known. Stewart Island Shags frequent rocky coasts and coastal waters of the south-eastern South Island. Fish, crabs, octopuses and polychaete worms are eaten. These shags nest in colonies on sea cliffs and small islands from North Otago to Foveaux Strait and around Stewart Island. The nest itself, on bare rock, 1–1.5 m tall and 0.5 m across, is a mound of vegetable matter (twigs, grass, peat, seaweed), cemented with excrement.

Pelicans, Gannets, Cormorants and Allies 65

Left: A colony of Stewart Island Shags at Taiaroa Heads.

Below: Pied and bronze forms of the Stewart Island Shag.

Stewart Island Shag.

Chatham Island Shag

Leucocarbo onslowi (Forbes, 1893)
[Outlying islands only]
Found only on the Chatham Islands, this shag feeds in adjacent coastal waters, eating mainly small fish from deep water. It is similar to the King Shag but smaller. It nests in colonies on small islets and on rocky headlands. The nests are usually close to the high-tide level on sloping, bare rocks, and they are made of plant material. The Chatham Island Shag is named for the fourth Earl of Onslow (1853–1911), who was Governor of New Zealand, 1888–92.

Auckland Island Shag

Leucocarbo colensoi (Buller, 1888)
[Outlying islands only]
These shags are found only at the Auckland Islands, where they frequent sheltered inlets and harbours as well as foraging far out to sea. The population is probably fewer than 1000 pairs, but as with the other shags of the New Zealand sub-antarctic islands, there are no apparent or immediate threats to their survival. This species lacks caruncles at the base of the bill. It is named after Reverend William Colenso (1811–99), a naturalist and missionary in New Zealand.

Bounty Island Shag

Leucocarbo ranfurlyi (Ogilvie–Grant, 1901)
[Outlying islands only]
This shag is unique to the Bounty Islands, a small group of wind- and wave-swept rocks lacking soil, fresh water and vegetation, some 800 km south-east of Dunedin. They feed in coastal waters and in the open ocean near their island group, sometimes in large feeding flocks. The population probably numbers about 600 pairs. They nest colonially, mainly on rock ledges, making nests out of seaweed. This species lacks caruncles at the base of the bill. It is named in honour of the fifth Earl of Ranfurly (1856–1933), Governor of New Zealand from 1897 to 1904, who collected or obtained New Zealand birds for the British Museum (Natural History) including the specimens from which this shag was described.

Campbell Island Shag

Leucocarbo campbelli (Filhol, 1878)
[Outlying islands only]
This species is endemic to Campbell Island where the population is thought to number 8000 birds. They are sometimes solitary; more usually gregarious in flocks of up to 2000 birds. These shags often feed in groups diving synchronously to chase marine invertebrates and small shoaling fish. The nesting colonies are on ledges along exposed, sheer cliffs. This species lacks caruncles at the base of the bill.

Pelicans, Gannets, Cormorants and Allies

A Spotted Shag at its nest.

Spotted Shag

(Parekareka)

Stictocarbo punctatus (Sparrman, 1786)

The slender Spotted Shag, with its slim bill, has the most striking breeding dress of any New Zealand shag — a double crest, black and white striped head, bright green facial skin, black spots on its grey back and wings, and yellow feet. It is one of the world's most beautiful shags. Spotted Shags prefer the waters close to rocky seashores and are locally common at various suitable sites around New Zealand, particularly around South and Stewart Islands. They nest colonially on cliffs and rocky islets. Spotted Shags catch fish and planktonic crustaceans, mainly in deep water (more than 10 m depth), as much as 15 km from shore.

Top: Spotted Shag.

Above: A nesting colony of Spotted Shags.

Spotted Shags.

Pelicans (Family Pelecanidae)

Pelicans are very large water-birds with long, heavy bills that end in a hook. They have large throat pouches used to trap fish and crustaceans, and they often feed co-operatively in a group. Pelicans inhabit brackish and coastal waters as well as large inland lakes and rivers. There are seven living species of pelican, and the Australian Pelican (*Pelecanus conspicillatus*) is a rare straggler to New Zealand, having been reported four times since 1890.

New Zealand Pelican

Pelecanus novaezealandiae Scarlett, 1966
[Extinct]

Rare subfossil bones of a pelican have been found occasionally in New Zealand — at Lake Grassmere in Marlborough, and at four North Island sites (Karikari Peninsula, Motutapu Island, Lake Waikaremoana and Lake Poukawa). The skeleton from Poukawa is 3500–4500 years old. Bones from some other sites are younger and may post-date human arrival in New Zealand. The pelvis is broader, and some of the bones slightly larger than in the modern Australian Pelican, and so the New Zealand Pelican has been regarded by some as a distinct species. However, it and the Australian Pelican may be the same, and the few New Zealand bones may represent Australian stragglers rather than birds from a local population. More specimens are needed to settle the issue.

Pitt Island Shag

Stictocarbo featherstoni Buller, 1873
[Outlying islands only]

This shag is the Chatham Island counterpart of the Spotted Shag of the mainland but is slightly darker and stockier. It is seen at sea and in coastal waters all around the islands of the Chatham group. The breeding population is about 500 pairs, dispersed in small colonies (5–20 pairs) on coastal cliffs and rocky islets throughout the Chatham group. The egg-laying season is a long one, from August to December. This species is named in honour of Dr I.E. Featherston (1813–76) who was Superintendent of Wellington Province.

Herons, Ibises, Storks and Allies

(Order CICONIIFORMES)

These are mainly large birds, with long legs and bills adapted for hunting and fishing in shallow water or marshes.

Herons and Bitterns
(Family Ardeidae)

Herons and bitterns have a spear-shaped bill used to catch prey, especially fish and other aquatic animals. They are seldom found far from coastal or inland waters. Bitterns tend to have shorter necks and legs and heavier bodies than herons. They prefer a heavy cover of dense reeds, whereas herons are less secretive and may be seen in open areas. These birds fly strongly on their broad wings and the neck is retracted during flight. The long toes are unwebbed. Powder-down feathers in the plumage break down at the tips to produce a fine powder used in care of the plumage. Many species develop ornamental plumes on the head and body, especially during the breeding season.

New Zealand Little Bittern

Ixobrychus novaezelandiae (Potts, 1871)
[Extinct]

The New Zealand Little Bittern is an enigma. Less than twenty have been collected, all during the nineteenth century and all from Westland, except one from Lake Wakatipu. Reports from the North Island are regarded as dubious. One could happily accept that these birds were Little Bitterns (*I. minutus*) that had straggled here from Australia, except that the New Zealand specimens are larger than their Australian relatives and different in plumage. Subfossil bones from two North Island sites (a swamp site and a kitchen midden) probably belong to this species, reinforcing the notion that there was a distinct New Zealand form. The *Ixobrychus* group of bitterns are small, slender birds up to about 65 cm in total length when stretched out. At least a part of the plumage of all forms of little bittern is heavily streaked.

Diurnal Birds of Prey

(Order FALCONIFORMES)

The daytime birds of prey, or raptors, are predators or scavengers. They are characterised by long wings, tail and legs. The strong feet are armed with sharp talons for seizing and carrying prey or carrion. The short, broad bill is hooked for tearing flesh, and there is a fleshy 'cere' at the base of the upper part of the bill. The plumage is usually drab, with grey or brown predominating. Raptors have large eyes and excellent daytime vision. The hearing is acute but the sense of smell is poor as in most birds. Females are usually the larger sex, in contrast to the situation in most other birds. Raptors are found all around the world except in Antarctica.

Hawks and Eagles
(Family Accipitridae)

The hawks and eagles are the largest group of birds of prey, and they occur on all continents except Antarctica and exploit a wide range of habitats. They are all very similar in body-form. Most hunt live prey, but harriers feed extensively on carrion. Undigestible food remains (bones, fur, feathers, insect hard-parts) are regurgitated as pellets. Their brightest feather-colours are rufous or chestnut, never red, blue, green or yellow. Eggs of a clutch are laid at least two days apart and incubation starts with the laying of the first egg. This means that the first chick or chicks to hatch have a head start over their sibling/s. The last chick to hatch may die, especially when food is short.

Eyles' Harrier

Circus eylesi Scarlett, 1953
[Extinct]

Bones of Eyles' Harrier, which was much larger than our presently common Australasian Harrier (*C. approximans*), were found during the 1949 excavations at Pyramid Valley in North Canterbury. The species was described in 1953 by Ron Scarlett of the Canterbury Museum, and named after his colleague J.R. Eyles. Subfossil bones have been found at sites throughout both the North and South Islands, including Maori kitchen middens. Not much is known about this species. Harriers have a varied diet, including carrion and small live prey such as birds, lizards, fish and insects. The female Eyles' Harrier may have weighed as much as 3 kg.

Chatham Island Sea-eagle

Haliaeetus australis (Harrison and Walker, 1973)
[Extinct. Outlying islands only]

The Chatham Island Sea-eagle was described in 1973 from a small group of subfossil bones that had been collected on Chatham Island and presented to what is now the Natural History Museum, London, by H.O. Forbes in 1892. Remains have not been found in association with human sites. This bird was large, as sea-eagles go, and it may have been more closely related to sea-eagles of the Northern Hemisphere than to the White-breasted Sea-eagle (*H. leucogaster*) of Australia. Sea-eagles are capable of seizing fish that swim near the surface.

New Zealand Eagle

Harpagornis moorei Haast, 1872
[Extinct]

The New Zealand Eagle, sometimes called Haast's Eagle after Julius von Haast who gave it its Latin name, is the largest eagle known, and therefore the largest bird of prey. The skull measures about 150 mm from the occiput (back) to

A museum mock-up of the giant New Zealand Eagle.

the tip of the beak. Estimates are that the female had a wingspan of about 2.4 m and weighed about 14.5 kg; males had wingspans of about 2.1 m and weighed about 11.5 kg. New Zealand Eagles were up to 30 percent heavier than the South American Harpy, *Harpia harpyja*, the largest living eagle. The legs of New Zealand Eagles were very strong, with talons up to 75 mm long, but the wings were relatively short. The wings were probably shorter and broader than those of open-country eagles, and the tail was probably relatively long as is typical of forest eagles. Bones of this giant eagle are nowhere common but have been found widely in the South Island and southern half of the North Island. The difficult question of association with human sites is not yet proved unequivocally, but the youngest eagle bones may be only 500 years old, indicating that eagles and humans co-existed. Other eagle bones are estimated to be up to 30,000 years old. Haast described two species of eagle, one based on small bones which are now believed to represent the male. Only three complete skeletons are known; two found in the late nineteenth century are in the Otago Museum and the Natural History Museum (London), and the third, found in a cave near Nelson in 1989, is held by the Museum of New Zealand, Wellington. New Zealand Eagles are presumed to have preyed on other birds, especially moas. The presence of their bones, along with those of moas in swamp deposits, suggests that they may have attacked moas that had become trapped in mires. Some researchers believe they were capable of killing adult Giant Moas. As the top carnivore in the early New Zealand food chain the numbers of eagles would have been relatively few. Research suggests that the New Zealand Eagle was a forest eagle that waited on high branches for prey to pass by, and swept down between trees at great speed (perhaps up to 80 km/h) to strike its prey. It was not an eagle that soared on thermal updrafts. Other evidence suggests that they were common in open subalpine areas.

Falcons
(Family Falconidae)

There are about 60 species of falcons, kestrels and their allies. Falcons are fast and powerful fliers with pointed wings. They can catch their prey on the wing, either seizing another bird in flight or snatching an animal from the ground. Small prey may be eaten on the wing; larger prey is carried to a perch and may be plucked or skinned. Undigested fragments are regurgitated as a pellet. Falcons are almost worldwide in distribution.

A New Zealand Falcon and nest.

Diurnal Birds of Prey

Left: A six-week-old New Zealand Falcon. Females fledge when five weeks old. Males are smaller and fledge when four-and-a-half weeks old.

Below: A New Zealand Falcon in flight.

New Zealand Falcon

(Karearea)

Falco novaeseelandiae Gmelin, 1788

Probably once found throughout the country, the New Zealand Falcon is now reduced to rougher mountainous districts with a covering of bush or tussock grassland. It is rare in the North Island, especially north of Taupo. A population breeds on the subantarctic Auckland Islands, but the Chatham Island population died out during the nineteenth century. It is usually seen alone, or in pairs before breeding. In open habitats New Zealand Falcons nest on bluff or slip faces, or on the ground beside a fallen log, and the nest is a mere scrape. In forested areas they nest in tall trees, often in clumps of epiphytes growing on high branches. The eggs vary from pale buff to a deep reddish-chestnut. Females are heavier than males by about two-thirds. New Zealand Falcons occasionally take large prey such as New Zealand Pigeons, Black-backed Gulls, ducks or herons, but most items are smaller, including birds, mammals (such as rabbits), lizards and large insects.

A New Zealand Falcon in typical South Island high-country habitat.

Rails, Cranes and Allies

(Order GRUIFORMES)

The gruiform birds are mainly ground-living birds, feeding and nesting on the ground. They have strong legs for walking and running, but many seldom fly and a few are flightless. Some, such as coots, are aquatic, while many inhabit marshes and the margins of water. Besides the rails and cranes the group includes the bustards, the Kagu of New Caledonia and various groups not found in the Australasian region. These birds are diverse in form yet all the evidence points to their relatedness.

Adzebills

(Family Aptornithidae)

This family contains just two species which are sometimes regarded as races of a single species. These large, flightless, rail-like birds, unique to New Zealand, have a distinctive jaw structure which sets them apart from the true rails. The jaw structure would have allowed a powerful grip with the tip of the bill. There are superficially resemblances between adzebills and the Kagus (*Rhynochetos* spp.) of New Caledonia, which also have their own family (Rhynochetidae), but the two may not be closely related. A study of adzebill skulls has suggested that adzebills are a sister-group of the galliform-anseriform birds (gamebirds and duck-like birds treated as a related group). If this is correct then adzebills may belong in a suborder of their own, making them about as distinctive a group as the moas.

The skull of adzebills is massive, with a thick-walled brain-case. The long, down-curved bill is stout and pointed with thick cutting edges. Small wing bones indicate that adzebills were flightless. They stood about 0.8 m tall. It is not clear whether adzebills were herbivores or carnivores. The chances are strong that they were omnivores, eating berries and leaves of soft herbaceous plants, as well as invertebrates (such as insects and spiders), and small vertebrates such as lizards. However, it has been suggested that they were specialist predators of reptiles including tuataras. There is some evidence that they preferred fairly open habitats as opposed to dense forest.

Rails, Gallinules and Coots
(Family Rallidae)

The cosmopolitan rails are predominantly water and swamp birds adapted to living in dense vegetation. They are small to medium-sized birds with long legs and toes, and spend most of their time on the ground. They are often secretive and skulking. The beak varies from short and conical to long and slender. The wings are generally short and rounded. Most species are reluctant to fly, and when they do the flight seems laboured. Some of these are still capable of long-distance colonisation. Many rails on predator-free, oceanic islands have become flightless. Rails are omnivores, though some are predominantly vegetarian.

North Island Adzebill

Aptornis otidiformis (Owen, 1844)
[Extinct]
A leg bone of the North Island Adzebill, collected about 1840 by a missionary in the East Cape area, was examined by Richard Owen, the famous British comparative anatomist, who wrongly described it in 1844 as a moa (*Dinornis otidiformis*). Subfossil bones of this species have since been found at many natural sites, but remains are rare in Maori kitchen middens. The weight is estimated to have been 10–11 kg.

South Island Adzebill

Aptornis defossor Owen, 1871
[Extinct]
The South Island Adzebill was larger than the North Island species, and probably reached 12–13 kg. Its bones have been found at numerous sites, both natural deposits and Maori kitchen middens.

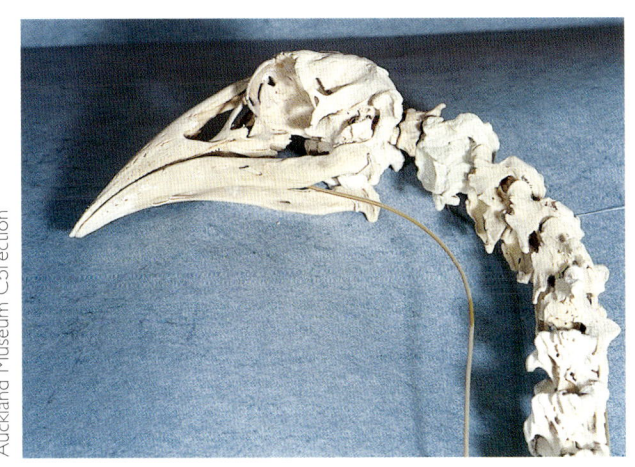

Head and neck bones of South Island Adzebill.

Dieffenbach's Rail

Gallirallus dieffenbachii (G.R. Gray, 1843)
[Extinct. Outlying islands only]
This flightless rail is known from one specimen collected by the German naturalist Ernst Dieffenbach (1811–55) in 1840 on Chatham Island (now at the Natural History Museum, Britain), and from bones found on Chatham and Pitt Islands in both natural sites and in Moriori kitchen middens. Dieffenbach's Rail is sometimes considered to be just a subspecies of the Banded Rail (*G. philippensis*), which occurs on the three main islands of New Zealand, and also in Australia and throughout the arc of islands from Indonesia and the Philippines to west Polynesia. However, research suggests that Dieffenbach's Rail is a distinct species. It was slightly larger than the Banded Rail, except for the wings. The two species are likely to have shared a common ancestor, and Dieffenbach's Rail probably arose from a population of ancestral Banded Rails that established after several flew to the Chathams from New Zealand. Dieffenbach's Rail had a fairly average bill shape for a rail and was probably a generalist feeder, like the Banded Rail. Dieffenbach 'often heard its shrill voice in the bush' and wrote that it 'was formerly very common, but since cats and dogs have been introduced it has become very scarce'.

Chatham Island Rail

Gallirallus modestus (Hutton, 1872)
[Extinct. Outlying islands only]
The Chatham Island Rail was discovered on tiny Mangere Island in the Chatham group by H.H. Travers in 1871. It also occurred on Chatham and Pitt Islands, as evidenced by subfossil bones, including some from probable Moriori kitchen middens. On these islands it probably died out in the early 1800s. The species persisted until about 1900 on Mangere from where most of the approximately 26 stuffed specimens in the museums of the world were collected. This bird probably declined as a result of Polynesian settlement. Then European settlement, which brought the introduction of cats to Mangere Island, clearance of the forest and the collecting of specimens for museums, dealt a final blow. The Chatham Island Rail, like Dieffenbach's Rail, probably arose from an invasion of the Chathams by

Banded Rails from New Zealand. Which of the two separate invasions was the earlier is debatable. The Chatham Island Rail probably weighed a little under 70 g (the weight of a Song Thrush, *Turdus philomelos*) — much smaller than Dieffenbach's Rail (*c.* 180 g). It had drab brown plumage which hung rather loosely. The wings and breast bone were so greatly reduced that this rail was flightless. The bill was slender, slightly downcurved and relatively long, which probably means it was a more specialised feeder than Dieffenbach's Rail. Early accounts indicate that the Chatham Island Rail was nocturnal, nested in holes in the ground and ate invertebrates, including beetles and amphipods. Only one egg was ever described (now in the Natural History Museum, Britain); it was 37 mm long and white with faint spotting. Subfossil bones of this rail fall into two broad size-classes which probably represent the male and female.

Chatham Island Rail.

Weka.

Weka

Gallirallus australis (Sparrman, 1786)

The Weka is a large, flightless rail with a stout bill and legs, and short, rounded wings. It once inhabited forest, scrub, swamp margins, sand-dunes, rocky shorelines and subalpine grassland throughout New Zealand, but it is now much reduced in distribution. On the mainland the Weka's main stronghold is parts of the northern half of the South Island. It is generally a shy bird, but near habitations or camp sites, bold, inquisitive individuals may become habituated to people to the extent that they may even damage or steal small items. Though it is one of New Zealand's most distinctive surviving endemic birds, and is absent from most of the mainland, ironically it is often a pest on island reserves where it may prey upon species of conservation interest such as reptiles, invertebrates, adult seabirds and eggs of ground-nesting birds. Wekas have had to be removed from many offshore islands to increase the prospects for other species. There are four subspecies of Weka which differ in coloration and vary a little in size. One subspecies, the Buff Weka, died out in its natural range in the eastern South Island, but it was introduced to the Chatham Islands where it is common in many areas and where harvesting for food is permitted. Wekas are most active in the late afternoon and evening. Adult Wekas remain in confined areas all year, but juveniles disperse. Wekas are capable of swimming across a kilometre of water. They are omnivorous, eating fallen fruits, grasses and seeds as well as invertebrates and lizards. They may damage planted vegetable seedlings and they readily kill small mammals such as rats and mice. Wekas are thought to have arisen from an early invasion of New Zealand by ancestral Banded Rails (*G. philippensis*) from Australia. Much more recently, Banded Rails have again established in New Zealand, and these are not yet greatly changed from the contemporary Australian birds.

Rails, Cranes and Allies 77

Left: Weka and nest.

Below: A newly hatched Weka chick peers from the safety of its parent's plumage.

Weka and chick.

Snipe-rail

Capellirallus karamu Falla, 1954
[Extinct]

The small, flightless Snipe-rail was very distinctive, having perhaps the longest bill and smallest wings (relative to body size) of any rail; the bill is twice as long as the brain-case. In body-size Snipe-rails were much the same size as Banded Rails. Subfossil bones have been found at numerous sites including Maori kitchen middens, but only in the North Island. The slightly down-curved bill was flexible, and the blunt, flattened tip was probably sensory, indicating adaptation for probing. Snipe-rails were probably forest birds and with their highly adapted probing bill they may have filled the ecological niche of a tiny kiwi.

Giant Chatham Island Rail

Diaphorapteryx hawkinsi (Forbes, 1892)
[Extinct. Outlying islands only]

The large, flightless Giant Chatham Island Rail is known from subfossil bones in sand-dune and Moriori midden sites on Chatham Island. The long, down-curved bill tapers to a point, and the leg bones are stout. The Giant Chatham Island Rail stood about 0.4 m tall, and weighed perhaps 2 kg — twice as much as a Weka (*Gallirallus australis*). Bones of this species were first collected in the late 1800s by Mr W. Hawkins, after whom the bird is named. Bones from some archaeological sites may be as recent as the eighteenth century AD, indicating that this rail co-existed with humans for several hundred years.

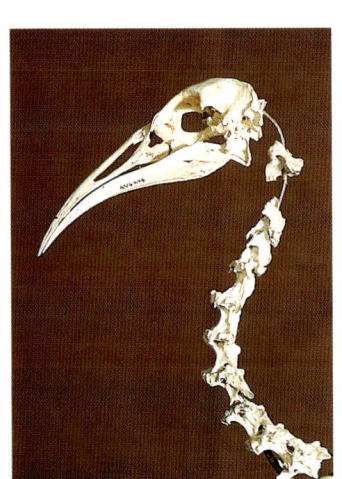

Head and neck bones of Giant Chatham Island Rail.

South Island Takahe.

North Island Takahe

Porphyrio mantelli (Owen, 1848)
[Extinct]

Subfossil bones of a takahe significantly taller than the South Island Takahe have been found in the North Island, some in Maori kitchen midden sites. A truly fossilised bone from the Pleistocene (up to two million years old) has been found at Napier. Although taller, the North Island Takahe may or may not have been heavier than the South Island species. The two kinds of takahe have usually been regarded as subspecies of the same species. Research, however, suggests not only that they are distinct species but that they may have arisen independently after separate colonisations of New Zealand by ancestors of the modern Pukeko (*P. porphyrio*). The North Island Takahe is named in honour of Walter Mantell (1820–95), naturalist, politician and founder of the New Zealand Institute, later the Royal Society of New Zealand.

South Island Takahe

Porphyrio hochstetteri (Meyer, 1883)

The South Island Takahe, or Notornis, is a giant flightless swamphen — the world's largest living rail — weighing 2–3 kg. The bill of swamphens extends onto the forehead as a shield. The shield and massive bill are scarlet in the Takahe as in the closely related Pukeko. Takahes are completely vegetarian, eating mainly leaf-bases of grasses and grass seeds in the alpine grasslands during summer. Nowadays Takahes have to compete with Red Deer for these foods. In winter, when the tussock grassland is snow-bound, Takahes move into adjacent forest to eat fern rhizomes and the like. The South Island Takahe is named after Ferdinand von Hochstetter (1829–84), an Austrian geologist who travelled widely in New Zealand. Between 1849 and 1898, four specimens of the South Island Takahe were seen or taken in the south-west of the South Island. Then the bird was thought to be extinct until a population was rediscovered west of Lake Te Anau in 1948.

Rails, Cranes and Allies

Despite the best efforts of conservation staff since then, Takahes remain in low numbers both in captivity and in the wild — in the Murchison and Stuart Mountains, and on several small islands where introduced.

Above: The Takahe is the world's largest living rail.

Above right: A Takahe chick on Tiritiri Matangi Island.

Right: Takahes liberated on Tiritiri Matangi Island in the Hauraki Gulf have bred successfully. Here, a parent feeds its chick.

Hodgen's Rail

Gallinula hodgeni (Scarlett, 1955)
[Extinct]
Remains of Hodgen's Rail, a flightless moorhen which had a short, wide bill, have been found at several sites in both the North and South Islands, including Maori kitchen middens. Hodgen's Rail was named after Messrs J. and R. Hodgen, owners of Pyramid Valley swamp where some of the bones were found. Hodgen's Rail probably weighed 400–500 g. It was roughly the size of the Australian Black-tailed Native-hen (*G. ventralis*), which is about 35 cm from bill to tail, though the latter flies and has longer, slimmer legs. The Black-tailed Native-hen has been recorded as a straggler in New Zealand, having flown the Tasman at least four times during the 1900s. Hodgen's Rail is probably descended from ancestors of the Black-tailed Native-hen that colonised New Zealand from Australia in the more distant past.

New Zealand Coot

Fulica prisca Hamilton, 1893
[Extinct]
Subfossil bones of this very large, flightless coot have been widely found in the North and South Islands at both natural sites and Maori midden sites. The Eurasian Coot (*F. atra*), which is widespread in Australia, was a rare straggler to New Zealand until the 1950s, when large numbers appeared and breeding was first recorded. Now it is widespread and increasing in New Zealand. The New Zealand Coot is probably derived from a much earlier colonisation of New Zealand by ancestors of *F. atra*. Research has suggested that this ancestral bird achieved its large size after colonising New Zealand, that it colonised the Chatham Islands (see next species) while still able to fly, and that both populations then became flightless. New Zealand Coots probably inhabited all types of freshwater habitats, eating water plants, seeds and invertebrate animals.

Chatham Island Coot

Fulica chathamensis Forbes, 1892
[Extinct. Outlying islands only]
The flightless Chatham Island Coot was slightly larger than the New Zealand Coot, and probably weighed about 1.3 kg. The two species differed in minor details of their bones. Depressions evident on the skull of most Chatham Island birds accommodated enlargement of the salt-excreting glands above the eyes, and this suggests that the birds were adapting to the saltiness of the Chatham Island lagoons. Chatham Island Coot bones have been found in both natural sites and in Moriori kitchen middens.

Waders, Gulls and Allies

(Order CHARADRIIFORMES)

The birds of this large and important group include the waders or shore-birds, and the gulls and terns. They are found throughout the world including arctic and antarctic regions. Charadriiforms are mainly ground-living and ground-nesting. Most live near water, either inland or at the shore, and prefer open areas where they rely on cryptic colours and alertness to avoid predators. Their bills are mostly adapted for probing in soft ground. In some the front toes are webbed. Most charadriiforms are strongly gregarious outside the breeding season, and many perform spectacular migrations. In many species both the eggs and the downy chicks are cryptically coloured for camouflage against sand, stones and other substrates.

Sandpipers and Snipes
(Family Scolopacidae)

This family includes the snipes, sandpipers, godwits and curlews. They have long, slender, flexible bills which, if desired, may be opened just at the tip to aid in the precise manipulation of small items of food. Most species have long legs, long necks, short tails and long, pointed wings. Snipes have particularly long bills and relatively short legs. They are skulking and cryptically coloured and the eyes are set well back on the head which gives a wide field of view. Snipes usually prefer open marshy habitats away from the shore, unlike other members of the family which are typical waders feeding on mudflats in large congregations. The endemic snipes of New Zealand are the only scolopacids in Australasia that breed locally and are not trans-equatorial migrants.

Chatham Island Snipe.

New Zealand Snipe

(Hakawai)
Coenocorypha aucklandica (G.R. Gray, 1845)
[Outlying islands only]

Holocene fossil bones show that a kind of snipe, probably this species, was once found throughout New Zealand. It very likely became extinct after Polynesian settlement, though to date there are no records from archaeological sites to prove this. In 1870 two snipes of this species were seen on Little Barrier Island, but none have been seen since. New Zealand Snipes died out on islands off Stewart Island, after predators reached them, and were last seen there in the 1960s. New Zealand Snipes nest on or near the ground and seldom fly; this makes them vulnerable to predators. Now, they are restricted to predator-free subantarctic islands where separate subspecies persist on the Snares Islands, Auckland Islands and Antipodes Island. In November 1997 snipes were discovered on a small island off Campbell Island — snipes were never before recorded in the Campbell group and they may prove to be a new subspecies of New Zealand Snipe. New Zealand Snipes avoid open areas and prefer dense ground-cover. On some islands the snipes give aerial displays at night, producing a ghostly whistle as air, passing through the fanned tail, causes the feathers to vibrate. They lay two eggs. The chicks leave the nest the day they hatch and a different parent looks after each one, remaining together for about nine weeks.

Chatham Island Snipe

Coenocorypha pusilla (Buller, 1869)
[Outlying islands only]

This species is smaller than the New Zealand Snipe, but similar in appearance and habits. It died out on the main Chatham Island but persists in good numbers on outer islands of the Chatham group, particularly South East Island. Chatham Island Snipes keep to forest and other dense cover by day, but at night they will forage in open areas. They give aerial displays at night (and like some populations of New Zealand Snipe, they produce sounds from their tail feathers) but fly by day only if disturbed at close range.

Giant Chatham Island Snipe

Coenocorypha chathamica (Forbes, 1893)
[Extinct. Outlying islands only]

Bones of the Giant Chatham Island Snipe, a species described and named in 1893, are known from both Moriori kitchen middens and natural sites. It once lived on Chatham Island itself and has been tentatively identified from Pitt and Mangere Islands. The Giant Chatham Island Snipe was much larger than the Chatham Island Snipe, a species whose bones are also found in subfossil and archaeological records. The beak of the giant species was 25 percent larger.

Oystercatchers
(Family Haematopodidae)

Oystercatchers are large, stout waders with thick legs and a long, solid bill, adapted for probing and for opening hard-shelled marine animals including chitons, limpets and bivalves. The plumage is black or pied, the bill bright orange-red, and the legs red or pink. Oystercatchers live mostly at the coast but some move inland to breed.

The endemic Variable Oystercatcher is the world's only oystercatcher with polymorphic plumage phases.

Two-day-old Variable Oystercatcher chicks.

Top: Variable Oystercatchers changing over during incubation.

Above: Shown on its nest, this Variable Oystercatcher is of the black plumage phase.

Variable Oystercatcher

(Torea)
Haematopus unicolor Forster, 1844

This is the largest oystercatcher in New Zealand, by a small degree. It is the world's only polymorphic oystercatcher, with three interbreeding plumage forms — black, pied and intermediate. The relative incidence of these forms varies geographically. Black birds (Maori name, Torea-pango) are the most numerous and their proportion of the total population increases southwards, with no other form present in Stewart Island, for example. Variable Oystercatchers prefer sandy or rocky shores, where they breed, and are uncommon in estuaries, even outside the breeding season. They occur sparingly throughout New Zealand on suitable coasts, typically seen in pairs during the breeding season. There is no pronounced migration. The total population numbers about 4000 birds.

Chatham Island Oystercatcher

Haematopus chathamensis Hartert, 1927
[Outlying islands only]

The Chatham Island Oystercatcher is one of the world's rarest waders with a population of about 100 birds. It is very like the pied phase of the Variable Oystercatcher but the beak is shorter and the legs and feet are thicker. They occur on rocky and sandy shores throughout the Chatham group. They often feed on rocky tidal platforms, especially at low tide when the intertidal zones are exposed. Chatham Island Oystercatchers do not migrate, and in fact seldom fly. Pairs have territories that they usually occupy and defend all year.

Stilts and Avocets

(Family Recurvirostridae)

A small family of slim, graceful waders remarkable for the relative length and slenderness of their bill, neck and legs. They have the longest legs (relative to their body size) of any birds except flamingos, and they will wade up to their underparts at the edges of freshwater, saltwater or brackish lagoons. The plumage is predominantly black and white.

Black Stilt

(Kaki)

Himantopus novaezelandiae Gould, 1841

Of the seven or so species of stilts and avocets around the world this is the only black one. It is also one of the rarest waders in the world with a population of about 100, including those in captivity. New Zealand has a second species of stilt, the cosmopolitan Pied Stilt, *H. himantopus*, which was absent (or rare) until the first record in 1854. Having established, presumably from Australia, it eventually became our commonest stilt. It is likely that the Black Stilt descends from a population of the ancestral Pied Stilt that established in New Zealand many millennia ago and began evolving in isolation. Darkening of the plumage is one of the directions in which New Zealand birds have often evolved. The Black Stilt is

Black Stilt.

Left: A hybrid Black Stilt with predominantly black plumage.

Below: A Black Stilt on a freshwater lagoon.

slightly larger than the Pied in most measurements, except neck and leg length. Unlike Pied Stilts, Black Stilts have lost certain distraction displays, they breed solitarily, and their chicks are longer in the nest. The physical and behavioural differences between the two have not been sufficient to prevent the species interbreeding. As well as suffering from predation and habitat loss, the Black Stilt is in danger of hybridising out of existence. The hybridising testifies to the similarity of the two species and to the recency of their separation. If the ancestral Black Stilts had arrived earlier, or the modern Pied Stilts had not arrived until the distant future, then the Black Stilt may have become too dissimilar to hybridise — probably larger and less able to fly. The juvenile Black Stilt has a white head, neck and breast, but this changes gradually to black during the first year. Black Stilts breed near fresh water in the Mackenzie Basin, inland South Canterbury, and disperse more widely after breeding. This is a relict distribution, and during the 1800s they bred in both main islands.

A hybrid Black Stilt with Pied Stilts.

Plovers, Dotterels and Lapwings
(Family Charadriidae)

The names plover and dotterel are used interchangeably in New Zealand. These small waders have a rounded, plump body with short legs and a short bill and tail. The bill is shorter than the head and is adapted for picking invertebrates from the surface, often from wet sand or mud. When feeding, they characteristically 'walk and stop' or 'run-stop-peck'. There are about 65 species.

New Zealand Dotterel.

New Zealand Dotterel

(Tuturiwhatu)
Charadrius obscurus Gmelin, 1789

The New Zealand Dotterel is one of the largest of the world's dotterels. The population totals about 1400 birds. The northern population breeds at beaches and estuaries (stream mouths, low dunes, sandbanks, shellbanks) around the northern half of the North Island, particularly the east coast, and spends

New Zealand's **Unique Birds**

the rest of the year in much the same situation. The endangered southern population, numbering about 100 birds, breeds on open, subalpine hilltops and ridges in the centre of Stewart Island, and then migrates to the coast. Pairs space out and defend territories while breeding but form small flocks outside the breeding season. Non-breeding adults have pale underparts, but these become rufous during breeding, especially in males. New Zealand Dotterels probably once bred in suitable habitats all over New Zealand. Banding has shown that New Zealand Dotterels can live 30, perhaps 40, years.

Above left: After the autumn moult, male New Zealand Dotterels often display a bright orange breast.

Top right: A two-day-old New Zealand Dotterel chick.

Above right: Nests of the New Zealand Dotterel are sometimes decorated with shells.

It is unusual for New Zealand Dotterels to use nesting material. This nest is lined with grasses.

The chestnut breast band is more prominent in the male Banded Dotterel.

Banded Dotterel

(Tuturiwhatu)
Charadrius bicinctus Jardine and Selby, 1827

This small dotterel is New Zealand's most abundant member of the plover family. The winter population in New Zealand is about 7500 birds. It is found throughout New Zealand, and breeds at the coast on sandy beaches and shellbanks, or inland on shingle riverbeds and river terraces. In winter, most Banded Dotterels migrate — either to Australia, to northern New Zealand, or from inland to the coast. Banded Dotterels are therefore endemic to New Zealand only in terms of their breeding distribution. It seems that more than half the population migrates to Australia, where they are called Double-banded Plovers, and these birds are mainly those that breed in the South Island high country. Those breeding in the Canterbury lowlands and the northern part of the South Island tend to winter in northern New Zealand. There is a small population of slightly larger birds resident at the Auckland Islands.

90 New Zealand's **Unique Birds**

Left: Banded Dotterel. A distraction display draws attention away from the nest.

Below: Three eggs usually form the Banded Dotterel's clutch.

Above: Banded Dotterel chicks are mobile soon after hatching.

Right: A female Banded Dotterel incubating.

Waders, Gulls and Allies

Below: A Shore Plover is well camouflaged on a marine rock platform, where the birds generally feed.

Wrybill.

Shore Plover

(Tuturuatu)
Thinornis novaeseelandiae (Gmelin, 1789)
[Outlying islands only]
In 1773 this plover was recorded in the South Island at Dusky and Queen Charlotte Sounds but it quickly died out, presumably because of the introduction of Norway rats and feral cats. There are no verified North Island records, but Shore Plovers probably occurred all around the New Zealand coast. Now they are restricted to the Chatham Islands where there are less than 150, largely confined to South East Island. Shore Plovers inhabit saltmeadows and rocky wave platforms. An attempt in the 1990s to establish (or 're-establish') Shore Plovers in the Hauraki Gulf near Auckland, by releasing captive-reared birds, may not have succeeded. There is evidence of a close relationship between the Shore Plover and the Hooded Plover, *Charadrius rubricollis*, of Australia, so much so that the Australian species has been moved to the genus *Thinornis*. They share the same sort of beach-strand habitat and both lack a non-breeding plumage.

Wrybill

(Ngutuparore)
Anarhynchus frontalis Quoy and Gaimard, 1830
This small plover is the world's only bird with a beak curved to one side. The end third of the beak curves to the bird's right, and is used to extract aquatic invertebrates from beneath stones at the water's edge in their inland South Island breeding habitat. On the wet silty mud of North Island estuaries they catch marine crustaceans and the like by a scything or spooning movement of the bill across the mud surface. Wrybills also peck and probe in search of food. They nest on braided, shingle riverbeds in Canterbury and Otago, where the adults, eggs and chicks are all beautifully camouflaged against the grey-

New Zealand's Unique Birds

Left: Wrybills in flight.

Below: Wrybills nest on the shingle banks of South Island rivers.

coloured greywacke stones. Most wrybills winter in the estuaries of the northern half of the North Island — especially the Manukau and Kaipara Harbours and the Firth of Thames. This migration is similar to that carried out by a segment of the population of Banded Dotterels. Pairs are solitary and secretive while breeding, but wrybills are highly gregarious in the non-breeding season, forming large flocks. A flock in flight seen from a distance is often a spectacular sight, appearing to move like a 'flung scarf'. Counts have shown that the winter population of wrybills is about 3500 birds.

Wrybills wait for the tide to recede so they can resume feeding on the exposed mudflats.

Gulls and Terns
(Family Laridae)

Gulls and terns are common and widespread, terns all over the world, and gulls everywhere except in the tropical belt. They usually prefer coastal situations near the shore. Most gulls and terns are gregarious, feeding in flocks and nesting in colonies near water. Terns (or 'sea-swallows') are more aerial and more dainty than gulls, with narrower, more pointed wings and usually a deeply forked tail. The adaptation of terns to an aerial lifestyle is shown by their relatively short legs and small feet. Unlike gulls, their progress on land is limited to an inefficient shuffle.

Black-billed Gulls.

From an early age chicks congregate in a crèche and are protected from predation by a few adult Black-billed Gulls.

Top: A Black-billed Gull's nest on a South Island riverbed.

Above: Black-billed Gull. Incubation is shared by both parents.

Black-billed Gull

Larus bulleri Hutton, 1871

The Black-billed Gull is superficially very similar to the Red-billed Gull, *Larus novaehollandiae*, a species New Zealand shares with Australia and South Africa. The Black-billed Gull is unusual in being essentially an inland gull. They breed mainly on the braided, gravel riverbeds of the South Island, but some breed at sites around the North Island coast and inland at a few North Island localities including Lake Rotorua. Those that breed inland generally move to the coast during winter. Numbers appear to have increased during the latter decades of the twentieth century. Near their South Island breeding colonies they feed at wet and recently ploughed fields and have to this extent benefited from the spread of arable farming. Black-billed Gulls take a wide variety of invertebrate prey items. They are more specialised feeders than Red-billed or Black-backed Gulls (*L. dominicanus*) and are adept at catching prey that is on the wing or at the water surface. They are the least likely of the three New Zealand gulls to scavenge around human settlements. Named after Buller (see Buller's Shearwater).

Waders, Gulls and Allies

Black-fronted Tern

(Tarapiroe)
Sterna albostriata (G.R. Gray, 1845)

This is yet another species that breeds on the riverbeds of the eastern South Island (see Black Stilt, Banded Dotterel, Wrybill, Black-billed Gull). Like the Black-billed Gull, it is unusual in being an inland-breeding larid, rather than a coastal-breeding one. Black-fronted Terns breed in colonies much as Black-billed Gulls do, and the two species often nest nearby. Like the gulls, Black-fronted Terns have benefited from the presence of arable farmland close to the breeding colonies from which earthworms and grubs can be readily obtained, especially after rain or ploughing. Black-fronted Terns are mainly a South Island bird, but in winter they disperse widely around New Zealand, especially along the east coast of the South Island and in the Cook Strait area. They are gregarious, often seen in flocks. They feed at the coast — in estuaries, river mouths and harbours — and at sea within 10 km of the shore. The black cap of breeding adults gives way to a mottled plumage after breeding.

Top: Black-fronted Terns nest on South Island shingle riverbeds.

Above: Black-fronted Tern.

A Black-fronted Tern at its nest.

Pigeons and Doves

(Order COLUMBIFORMES, Family Columbidae)

Pigeons are plump birds with small heads, dense plumage and short legs and bills. The feathering extends further down the leg than in most birds. They are strong, direct fliers with rounded wings. Pigeons are herbivores with a crop that distends to allow gorging. The nest is a flimsy, unlined platform of twigs, and the eggs are white. For their first few days the sole food of nestling pigeons is a fluid ('crop-milk') regurgitated by both parents. It is highly nutritious and forms when cells from the epithelium, which lines the crop, proliferate and slough off. There are some 300 species of pigeons.

New Zealand Pigeon feeding on nikau fruit. The birds play an important ecological role with the dispersal of seeds for regeneration of native forests.

Pigeons and Doves 97

New Zealand Pigeons.

New Zealand Pigeon.

New Zealand Pigeon

(Kereru)

Hemiphaga novaeseelandiae (Gmelin, 1789)

The New Zealand Pigeon belongs in a group of mainly tropical fruit-pigeons, and they are large birds weighing about 650 g. New Zealand Pigeons are unusual in only rarely feeding in flocks. They eat leaves, buds, flowers and fruit. They swallow fruits whole and void the seeds intact, thus playing an important role — as with all fruit-pigeons — in dispersing forest tree seeds. In many areas where Kokakos are absent, New Zealand Pigeons are the only bird now capable of dispersing certain fruits — such as karaka, tawa and miro — too large to be eaten by other birds. Various extinct species like moas and adzebills probably helped to spread these seeds in the past. New Zealand Pigeons are found in native lowland forest, especially podocarp hardwood forest, and in bush remnants, city parks and large gardens. Outside the breeding season they travel long distances to visit favoured food sources.

New Zealand Pigeon bringing a stick to its nest.

New Zealand Pigeon. In the later stages of growth the chick is fed increasing amounts of fruit pulp and whole fruit.

They are strong fliers, and engage in spectacular aerial display flights during the breeding season. New Zealand Pigeons declined at the beginning of the 1900s with forest clearance and hunting, but their numbers increased after they were protected in 1921. Now they are under threat again from illegal hunting, predation at the nest and competition for food with Brushtail Possums. The New Zealand Pigeon had a counterpart on Norfolk Island (*H. spadicea*, the Norfolk Island Pigeon), which seems to have been exterminated by hunting and was not seen after 1900. The New Zealand, Norfolk Island and Chatham Island Pigeons are often treated as subspecies (which means, incidentally, that the New Zealand Pigeon is strictly not endemic to New Zealand), but each probably deserves specific status.

Chatham Island Pigeon

(Parea)
Hemiphaga chathamensis (Rothschild, 1891)
[Outlying islands only]

This is one of the world's rarest pigeons, which declined to a low of about 40 birds in 1990, but which is now increasing, aided by predator control and other interventions. The Chatham Island Pigeon was initially described as a separate species, but for a long time it was regarded as just a subspecies of the New Zealand Pigeon. Recent research has now demonstrated, however, that it is distinct enough to be regarded once again as a full species (Millener and Powlesland, in preparation). Chatham Island Pigeons are larger than their mainland counterpart — about one and a quarter times heavier — and there are plumage differences. They used to be widespread in the Chatham Islands but are now found mostly in forest in southern parts of the main island.

Parrots and Cockatoos

(Order PSITTACIFORMES)

Parrots typically have bright, colourful plumage, but the New Zealand members are rather drab, being mainly greenish or brownish. The beak is hooked and directed downwards so that parrots appear to be 'snub-nosed'. The upper part of the beak is hinged at the base and parrots can crack tough seeds with ease. The nostrils are enclosed in a fleshy 'cere'. The short, strong legs (and the beak) are useful for climbing, and the strong toes are arranged with two directed forwards and two backwards (a condition called zygodactyly). Most parrots are gregarious and lay white eggs in holes or crevices. They are mainly tropical and found mostly in the Southern Hemisphere. The division of parrots into subgroups is unsettled and much debated.

Parrots and Lorikeets
(Family Psittacidae)

The cockatoos, corellas and the Cockatiel — a group centred on Australia and New Guinea — seem to form a natural group (family Cacatuidae). The remaining majority of parrots (more than 300 species), including all New Zealand parrots, are in the current state of knowledge best put together in the Psittacidae. The Kakapo belongs in its own subfamily (Strigopinae; subfamilies end in -inae, families in -idae), as do the Kaka and the Kea (Nestorinae), which have spine-tipped tail feathers and a cockatoo-like flight and gait. The New Zealand parakeets belong in the Platycercinae along with the rosellas.

Male Kakapo.

Kakapo

Strigops habroptilus G.R. Gray, 1845

The Kakapo is the heaviest parrot in the world, the only flightless parrot, and one of only three terrestrial species. It is also unusual among parrots in being solitary, nocturnal, and in having an owl-like facial disc of hair-like feathers. It is one of the world's rarest parrots. Kakapos are the only New Zealand bird, flightless bird or parrot with a 'lek' (or arena) breeding system. The breeding male Kakapo broadcasts loud, repetitive, booming calls from a 'track-and-bowl' system that he has cleared on a prominent ridge-top. The calls attract females for mating; females nest near or far from the arena and tend the nest alone. The population breeds only every three to five years, depending on the periodic fruiting of various trees and other plants — Kakapos are strict herbivores. Kakapos feed on the ground or by clambering up shrubs and trees. They use their wings for balance as they climb and to break their fall as they descend to the ground. Males weigh about 2 kg (up to 4 kg), 20–50 percent more than females (around 1.5 kg). This is the biggest sexual size difference of any parrot. The nocturnal habits and camouflaging plumage of Kakapos were presumably a defence against raptors like the extinct New Zealand Eagle. Found throughout New Zealand up to the early period of Maori settlement, Kakapos were still in the central North Island and much of the South Island at the time of European settlement. They declined rapidly after stoats were introduced in the 1880s. During the 1980s and 1990s the last Kakapos were moved from Stewart Island to three predator-free island sanctuaries — Little Barrier, Maud and Codfish Islands. The current population is about 50 birds.

Parrots and Cockatoos 101

Above: A Kakapo in its 'bowl' at night.

Above right: A Kakapo feeding on flax seeds.

Right: The male Kakapo is heavier, with a larger bill and broader head, than the female.

North Island Kaka.

Kaka

Nestor meridionalis (Gmelin, 1788)

This large and vocal forest parrot weighs about 500 g, with males a little heavier than females. The plumage is brownish and rather drab, except for the underwings and rump which are crimson. North and South Island populations differ sufficiently to be regarded as separate subspecies. South Island birds are slightly bigger and have a paler crown. The Norfolk Island Kaka (*N. productus*), extinct since the mid-1800s, is closely related to the New Zealand form and sometimes regarded as a subspecies of it. Kakas nest in hollow branches or trunks, so they need forest with mature trees. However, they are strong fliers and will leave the bush to wander to bush remnants and well-treed towns and suburbs. Kakas eat seeds and fruits, but in so doing they crush the seeds and do not disperse them. They have a brush-tipped tongue that they use to lap nectar, honeydew and sap. They also eat insects, especially wood-boring grubs which they extract from live or decaying wood using their powerful beak. The future of Kakas on the mainland is uncertain in the face of predation by mammals and competition for food from possums and wasps.

Top right: A North Island Kaka feeding on a shrub.

Centre right: A female Kaka about to leave its nesting hole in a puriri tree trunk.

Right: Approximately every 80–90 minutes the male Kaka calls the incubating female from the nest to feed her by regurgitating vegetable food.

Kea

Nestor notabilis Gould, 1856

Keas are one of the world's few alpine parrots. They are prominent birds in their habitat with their loud, ringing call, their large size, boldness and scarlet underwings. Keas are gregarious and feed together on berries and shoots. Some have learnt to eat carrion, including dead sheep, and a few may injure sick, wounded, or even healthy sheep, by using their beaks to dig into the flesh on the sheep's back. Their reputation as sheep killers was probably largely undeserved, yet thousands were killed up until 1970, when they were given some legal protection. The Kea and Kaka are presumably alpine and lowland derivatives of the same ancestral stock. The Kea is larger than the Kaka at around 900 g. The Kea is now found only in South Island high country, mostly above 760 m, although they descend to lower altitudes at times of heavy snowfall. Subfossil bones have been found at one North Island site, showing that they once occurred more widely.

Above: Keas inhabit alpine and beech forests only in the South Island.

Left: An immature Kea, showing the yellow-coloured cere and eye ring.

Yellow-crowned Parakeet

(Kakariki)
Cyanoramphus auriceps (Kuhl, 1820)

This small, green parrot with yellow and red markings on the head, is found in the larger tracts of native forest throughout much of New Zealand and on the Auckland Islands. A second subspecies (Forbes' Parakeet, *C. auriceps forbesi*) occurs on the Chatham Islands, and is slightly larger. The mainland subspecies (*C. auriceps auriceps*) is uncommon, while Forbes' Parakeet is in very low numbers and threatened by hybridisation with Red-crowned Parakeets (*C. novaezelandiae*) in part of its range where the habitat is disturbed. In undisturbed habitats the Yellow-crowned Parakeet prefers taller forest and scrub, with less open ground, than does the slightly larger Red-crowned Parakeet. 'Yellow-crowns' tend to eat more invertebrates and less vegetable matter than 'red-crowns'.

Above left: A Kea in flight, revealing its scarlet underwing.

Below left: Yellow-crowned Parakeet.

Above right: Yellow-crowned Parakeets often feed on the ground, leaving them vulnerable to predation from feral cats and mustelids.

Antipodes Island Parakeet.

Antipodes Island Parakeet

Cyanoramphus unicolor (Lear, 1831)
[Outlying islands only]

This is the largest *Cyanoramphus* parakeet at about 130 g, and the only one that lacks red or yellow markings on the head — the plumage is entirely green except for some blue on the wings. It occurs only on Antipodes Island and its islets. Antipodes Island Parakeets number several thousand and at present there are no threats to their survival. They nest on the ground by burrowing into the bases of tall tussocks or into fibrous peat accumulated under a cover of vegetation. The burrows are sometimes over a metre long. Antipodes Island Parakeets fly well but spend much of their time clambering through vegetation and moving over the ground on foot. They are predominantly vegetarian but also scavenge carrion around penguin colonies. Antipodes Island Parakeets most likely share a common ancestor with the Red-crowned Parakeet (*C. novaezelandiae*), which is also present on the Antipodes (as an endemic subspecies known as Reischek's Parakeet, *C. n. hochstetteri*). The ancestral population of the Antipodes Island Parakeet colonised the Antipodes from mainland New Zealand and gave rise to a species that is larger and duller than the mainland form. This mirrors, on a smaller scale, the tendencies that birds have shown in colonising mainland New Zealand from Australia — the trend for the birds to become large and drab. Reischek's Parakeet represents a second, more recent invasion by Red-crowned Parakeet stock. This is the same sort of double invasion that on the mainland has produced such pairs of species as the Takahe and Pukeko. The two parakeets hybridise in captivity but this has never been noted on the Antipodes.

Cuckoos and Allies

(Order CUCULIFORMES, Family Cuculidae)

Traditionally the turacos of Africa have been placed with the cuckoos, but research suggests the two groups are not closely related, leaving the cuckoo family in its own order. They are mainly tropical. Those that breed in temperate areas migrate to the tropics outside the breeding season. With their pointed wings and long tails, cuckoos look rather hawk-like in flight. They are strong fliers and many are long-distance migrants. They have zygodactylous toes like parrots — two toes point forward, and two backwards. There are several groups, including the typical nest-building cuckoos, the anis, the group to which the Roadrunner *Geococcyx* belongs, the couas and the coucals. Those belonging to the subfamily Cuculinae are brood-parasites. They do not build a nest or rear their own young. Instead the female lays her small eggs individually in the nests of smaller insectivorous birds and plays no further part in the process. The cuckoo egg hatches quickly and the cuckoo chick grows rapidly, usually ejecting from the nest any eggs or other nestlings. Being larger than the foster-parents' own chicks, it needs to monopolise all the food they can bring. Parasitic cuckoos have simple, monotonous calls which must be innate since the young have no opportunity to learn the calls from their parents.

Long-tailed Cuckoo

(Koekoea)
Eudynamys taitensis (Sparrman, 1787)
This cuckoo makes a spectacular trans-oceanic annual migration to distant Pacific islands. It is a medium-sized cuckoo with an exceptionally long tail. It breeds only in New Zealand but spends the southern winter dispersed through a huge arc of islands from Micronesia and the Bismarck Archipelago (of Papua New Guinea) in the west, to the Marquesas and Tuamotus (of French Polynesia) in the east. The main wintering ground is from Fiji to the Society Islands. In New Zealand, Long-tailed Cuckoos are found in native forest throughout the country where they parasitise three closely related song birds — the Whitehead in the North Island, and the Yellowhead and Brown Creeper in the South Island. These cuckoos eat large insects and spiders. They are also predators of lizards and small birds, and occasionally eat berries and fruit.

Cuckoos and Allies 107

Left: A Long-tailed Cuckoo.

Below: Migrating Long-tailed Cuckoos are sometimes killed when they fly into reflecting windows.

Long-tailed Cuckoo. The very long tail of this species is most obvious in flight.

Owls

(Order STRIGIFORMES)

This group comprises the typical owls (see below) and the barn owls (family Tytonidae). They are predators with short, hooked beaks, and strong legs armed with talons. Owls hunt mostly at night. They have short tails, rounded wings, and big heads with large forward-facing eyes encircled by a wide facial disc. The plumage is soft and dense. Owls are light relative to their wing area and they are able to fly buoyantly with little flapping. They have acute hearing and excellent vision in poor light.

Typical Owls
(Family Strigidae)

The typical owls are found on all continents except Antarctica, and on many oceanic islands. They are mainly non-migratory and territorial. Most are nocturnal, roosting by day in holes or in thick foliage where their protective plumage makes them hard to see. They eat large insects and small vertebrates, which are coarsely dismembered or swallowed whole. Indigestible parts are regurgitated as pellets. Nests are usually in holes or hollows, and the rounded eggs are white. There are about 150 species.

Laughing Owl.

Laughing Owl

(Whekau)

Sceloglaux albifacies (G.R. Gray, 1844)

[Extinct]

The Laughing Owl was about twice as big as a Morepork (*Ninox novaeseelandiae*) and had longer legs, even allowing for size. It was the largest predatory nocturnal bird in New Zealand. It once occurred throughout the three main islands: bones have been found at numerous subfossil sites including Maori kitchen middens. In historical times the Laughing Owl was known in the North Island from only two museum skins and from two reliable sightings. The skins were collected near Mt Egmont in 1854 and from Wairarapa about 1868 (both are now lost), and the sightings were at Waikohu near Gisborne in 1889 and near Porirua before 1892. In the South Island the Laughing Owl was widely recorded in Nelson, Canterbury, Otago, Fiordland and on Stewart Island, but declined rapidly after about 1880. The last known specimen was found dead in July 1914 at Blue Cliffs, South Canterbury. The Laughing Owl was first described in 1844 from a specimen obtained at Waikouaiti near Dunedin. The bird was then fairly common, but relatively few were collected for museums and 40 years after discovery it was virtually gone. Two captive birds in Britain each weighed about 600 g when examined by G.D. Rowley in the 1870s. Rowley wrote: 'More gentle animals could not be; they allow themselves to be handled without any resentment.' Laughing Owls were mainly forest birds, but the last individuals recorded in the South Island frequented forest edges and rocky areas in open country. They were strictly nocturnal and may have been largely ground-feeders. Laughing Owls were generalist feeders — their known foods were bats, rodents, small and medium-sized birds, lizards, frogs, fish, earthworms and insects such as beetles. In some forested areas they caught nocturnal, ground-nesting seabirds, such as shearwaters and prions. The name 'laughing owl' refers to the weird call, said by T.H. Potts to be a 'loud cry, made up of a series of dismal shrieks frequently repeated'. A few nests lined with dry grass were found in crevices among rocks. The usual clutch was two eggs. The eggs were about 50 mm by 40 mm, and pure white, as is typical of owl eggs.

Frogmouths and Nightjars
(Order CAPRIMULGIFORMES)

These are nocturnal birds with cryptically coloured plumage that makes them difficult to see when they are resting by day. Nightjars (family Caprimulgidae; called goatsuckers and nighthawks in North America) are widely distributed around the world, there are many species and they often occur in large numbers. Frogmouths (family Podargidae), a smaller group, are restricted to Asia and the Australasian area, and occur in low numbers. There are several other families, including the owlet-nightjars (see below).

Owlet-nightjars
(Family Aegothelidae)

Owlet-nightjars are like small, long-tailed owls. They occur mainly in New Guinea, with single species reaching Australia, the Moluccas (Indonesia), New Caledonia and formerly New Zealand. The plumage is mottled brown and cryptic. The bill is extremely short and the gape wide. Owlet-nightjars have large eyes, some long stiff hair-like feathers on the face, and an owl-like stance. They prey on insects and other arthropods. Nesting is in a tree hollow or cleft, or in a tunnel in a bank. The eggs are round and white. Owlet-nightjars usually roost by day in tree-holes.

New Zealand Owlet-nightjar

Aegotheles novaezealandiae (Scarlett, 1968)
[Extinct]

This was the largest of all owlet-nightjars, with a weight of perhaps 200 g. The wing bones are not markedly larger than in modern species of owlet-nightjar, but the leg bones are much bigger, suggesting that it was flightless, or nearly so. It probably stood very upright on its long, thin legs. New Zealand Owlet-nightjars were presumably nocturnal. Subfossil bones have been recovered from many sites in both the North and South Islands. South Island specimens tend to be slightly larger than those from the north. Although a few bones of this species were collected in the nineteenth century, the New Zealand Owlet-nightjar was not described until 1968. Bones of this species are well represented in cave sites, suggesting that it habitually roosted in such places during the day. It may well have nested in caves too. It probably also roosted and nested in tree-holes. New Zealand Owlet-nightjars probably ate insects, other invertebrates and possibly nocturnal geckos (a type of lizard).

Passerine Birds
(Order PASSERIFORMES)

Over half of the nearly 10,000 living species of birds are passerine or 'perching' birds. Included in the order Passeriformes are most of the smallish singing birds, such as sparrows, thrushes and honeyeaters, that live in or around trees and bushes. Their feet, with three toes running forward and a fourth toe opposed, are adapted for gripping a perch. At hatching the young are blind, more or less naked and helpless.

Evidence is mounting that the passerine birds arose in Gondwana. Circumstantial evidence for this is the great diversity of primitive passerines (like the New Zealand wrens) now present in the Southern Hemisphere. Direct evidence comes from recent fossil finds, especially the discovery at Murgon, southeast Queensland, Australia, of fossil fragments of two forms that appear to be passerines, dated at about 55 million years old. If correctly identified these are the oldest passerine fossils.

The passerines are divided into two subgroups, the suboscines and the oscines (songbirds).

Suboscines

The suboscine passerines do not have the highly developed vocal apparatus (syrinx) that characterises the oscines, and therefore cannot sing so well. They originated in South America and are found today mainly in the Americas, but several kinds live elsewhere, such as the pittas of Africa, Asia and Australia. Of special interest to us are the New Zealand wrens which are usually regarded as suboscines. However, some authorities have doubted that they belong with this group, and have suggested that they may form a separate third suborder of passerines.

New Zealand Wrens
(Family Acanthisittidae)

The small, drab New Zealand wrens, with their muted calls, have an inconspicuousness that belies their zoological importance. With the moas, kiwis and adzebills they share the distinction of being endemic to New Zealand at a higher level, probably, than that of the family. New Zealand wrens are thus among the 'most' endemic of all New Zealand birds. They superficially resemble the wrens of the Northern

Hemisphere, but the two groups are not closely related.

The New Zealand wrens radiated into a group of seven species. Three of these appear to have become extinct during the period between Maori and European settlement and are known only from bones. Two further species have died out since European settlement. Yaldwyn's Wren was the largest and the Rifleman is the smallest. Females are larger than males. New Zealand wrens differed slightly in the size and shape of their bill and they would have searched for their arthropod prey in different ways. Before the first humans arrived the New Zealand forest would have bustled with energetic little wrens.

The New Zealand wrens are characterised by rounded wings, greatly reduced tails, and rather long legs and toes. They were clearly evolving in the direction of flightlessness, and, indeed, four of the species (Stephens Island Wren, Yaldwyn's Wren, Grant-Mackie's Wren and the Long-billed Wren) are thought to have been flightless — the world's only flightless passerines.

Rifleman

(Titipounamu)

Acanthisitta chloris (Sparrman, 1787)

The Rifleman is the best-known New Zealand wren — sadly, only two species remain. It is New Zealand's smallest bird, with a total length of about 80 mm and an average weight of about 6.5 g, only one-third the weight of a House Mouse

The Rifleman is New Zealand's smallest bird, measuring only 80 mm long.

Above: The Rifleman feeds entirely on insects and grubs.

Above right: A Rifleman about to enter its nest in a small cavity in the trunk of a beech tree.

(*Mus musculus*). The thin bill is slightly upturned. Riflemen are found in the larger tracts of forest, especially beech forest, throughout the country. In some areas they use scrub and mature pine plantations. They move through the forest, usually in pairs or family groups, probing the trunks, branches and foliage, and giving their sharp, high-pitched calls. The enclosed nest is usually built in a tree-hole. Riflemen lay the eggs of their clutch two days (rather then one day) apart, and they are communal breeders — birds other than the parents (but usually young from a previous brood) may help to feed the young (see Whitehead, p. 131). These are very unusual features for passerines from a worldwide perspective, but they are more common among the passerines of the Australasian region.

Bush Wren

Xenicus longipes (Gmelin, 1789)
[Extinct]

The most recent bird extinction in New Zealand was the dying out of the Bush Wren, and its demise was realised in retrospect and attracted no public attention. It once occurred throughout New Zealand. The North Island subspecies (*X. l. stokesii*) is known in historical times from only three specimens — two collected in the Rimutaka Range about 1850 and one from Taupo. Subfossil bones show that it once occurred more widely in the North Island. The South Island race (*X. l. longipes*) was widespread at the time of European settlement, especially in mountain forest. Stead's Bush Wren (*X. l. variabilis*), named as a distinct subspecies by Edgar Stead in 1936, was found on islands off the south-west coast of Stewart Island. Bush Wrens may have been seen in the South Island as late as 1968, but there are no later substantiated records. By the 1960s Stead's Bush Wren was confined to Big South Cape Island off

Passerine Birds

A male Rock Wren in typical alpine habitat.

Bush Wren. *Auckland Museum Collection*

Stewart Island. An irruption of Ship Rats began on Big South Cape in 1962, the rats having apparently reached the island along the mooring lines of fishing boats. The island's wildlife declined rapidly as rat numbers increased. Before the wrens disappeared in 1967, the Wildlife Service transferred six to nearby rat-free Kaimohu Island. Two were seen on Kaimohu in 1972 but an inspection in 1977, and subsequent visits, revealed none. The Bush Wren was larger than the Rifleman and had particularly long legs, hence the Latinised name *longipes*. It was a weak flier.

Rock Wren

Xenicus gilviventris Pelzeln, 1867

Today, this wren is found only in the Southern Alps. However, it seems that it once occurred in the North Island too — bones believed to be from this species have been found in North Island caves, though it is difficult to tell Rock Wren bones from those of certain other wrens. Rock Wrens are alpine birds, living above the treeline at 900–2500 m in and about rockfalls, screes and areas of low scrub. In Fiordland they occur at lower altitudes in subalpine scrub. Adult Rock Wrens remain in their small home ranges all year. Their flight is weak and they get about mainly by hopping. In winter when snow covers

The female Rock Wren lacks the olive-green colouring of the male.

The Rock Wren has a small tail.

an area of rocks or scrub they are able to move about in gaps and crevices beneath the snow. The bulky, covered nest is usually in a crevice. In parts of Fiordland in the early decades of the 1900s it seems there was confusion as to whether birds observed were Rock Wrens or the now-extinct Bush Wrens. The confusion was such that it is even possible that the two are altitudinal or geographic variants of the same species. The issue is hard to settle now as there are very few specimens of either wren in museum collections, and because the Bush Wren was never studied in the field in the South Island mountains.

Stephens Island Wren

Traversia lyalli Rothschild, 1894
[Extinct]

The Stephens Island Wren, as the name suggests, was found historically on this one small island in the Cook Strait area. However, subfossil bones of this species have now been found at several sites on both the North and South Islands, demonstrating that the Stephens Island population was a relict of a formerly widespread species. The bones have been found at both lowland and high-country sites, implying wide ecological preferences. The wren was discovered, and soon after eliminated, by a lighthouse keeper's cat — perhaps the shortest interval between discovery and extinction of any animal. Late in 1894 one of the Stephens Island lighthouse keepers, David Lyall, retrieved from the cat about seventeen specimens of the wren, a dozen of which are still available in museums. Lyall twice saw the bird alive and was seemingly the only European to do so. They were said to live among rocks and run about like mice. The wings were short and rounded, the body plumage soft, loose and rail-like. Research has shown that the Stephens Island Wren had such reduced wings as to be totally flightless. The genus is named for Henry Travers (1844–1928), a bird collector and dealer, and the specific name commemorates David Lyall.

Grant-Mackie's Wren

Pachyplichas jagmi Millener, 1988
[Extinct]
Subfossil bones of this species (also called the North Island Stout-legged Wren) are known from several dune and cave sites in the North Island. It is similar to Yaldwyn's Wren, but smaller. It was probably flightless. The specific name (*jagmi*) is derived from the initials of Dr J.A. Grant-Mackie of the University of Auckland, a leading New Zealand palaeontologist.

Yaldwyn's Wren

Pachyplichas yaldwyni Millener, 1988
[Extinct]
Also called the South Island Stout-legged Wren, this is the largest and most robust New Zealand wren, with a weight estimated to have been about 50 g. Subfossil bones of this species have been found at several South Island sites, particularly caves. Isolated bones were collected as long ago as 1892, but the species was not described until 1988, by which time new excavations had uncovered almost complete skeletons. Both Yaldwyn's and Grant-Mackie's Wrens have relatively reduced wing bones, but extremely robust legs, suggesting that they spent much time on the ground and were probably flightless. The end toe bones are flat, rather than curved, like those of a ground-dwelling, rather than a perching, bird. There is evidence that Yaldwyn's Wren occurred in both lowland podocarp-broadleaf forest and in sub-alpine scrub. It is named for Dr J.C. Yaldwyn, former director of the National Museum, Wellington, who contributed to the study of New Zealand's extinct birds.

Long-billed Wren

Dendroscansor decurvirostris Millener and Worthy, 1991
[Extinct]
Subfossil bones of this wren have been found only in the north-west Nelson and Southland districts of the South Island. The first bone was found in a cave at Oparara in 1983. The long beak is down-curved, and this is the only New Zealand wren with a significantly curved beak. Its reduced sternum and wing bones indicate that it was flightless. The weight of the Long-billed Wren is estimated to have been about 30 g, less than for Yaldwyn's Wren but more than for the Stephens Island Wren. Long-billed Wrens had relatively short, thin legs, and enlarged neck vertebrae. These skeletal features suggest that it may have behaved like an Australian tree-creeper (Climacteridae), moving up and down tree trunks and branches, and over fallen logs, probing in crevices for food. The Latin name means 'tree-climber with a down-curved beak'.

Oscines (Songbirds)

The oscines (songbirds) are tremendously successful as indicated by their diversity — some 4600 species, the most diverse single group of birds. Those in the Northern Hemisphere fall fairly obviously into families based partly on the shape of their bills as adaptations for feeding. For example, the seed-eating 'sparrows' (Ploceidae) and 'finches' (Fringillidae) and the insect-eating 'warblers' (Sylviidae) and 'flycatchers' (Muscicapidae), are all untroublesome groupings. Songbirds of the greater Australasian region, however, have never sat properly in these families. Our common garden songster, the Grey Warbler, was put in the warbler family (Sylviidae), and the acrobatic Fantail in the flycatcher family (Muscicapidae) because their feeding behaviour and beak-shape suggested this.

However, there is an interesting phenomenon called convergent evolution that can confuse our attempts to classify organisms. Usually, species with similar structures are closely related and have each acquired their shared feature by descent from a common ancestor. However, natural selection may give unrelated animals similar structures if they exploit the environment in a similar way. A classic example is the streamlined body-shape and solid, rounded fins of the sharks (cartilaginous fish), ichthyosaurs (extinct reptiles) and dolphins (mammals), unrelated animals moulded by natural selection to a similar shape because swimming fast in the sea is (or was) a requirement of their way of life.

Studies of molecular biology (especially comparisons of the thermal behaviour of strands of DNA taken from representative species and mixed in pair-wise comparisons) have revolutionised the study of bird taxonomic relationships. Among the new findings is the remarkable and unsuspected notion that the world's songbirds fall into two major groups: the corvids (Parvorder Corvida) which originated in the Australian region, and the passerids (Parvorder Passerida) which arose elsewhere. The Grey Warbler is a corvid and the Old World warblers are passerids. Their similar bill-shapes have arisen independently as a result of convergence, not by descent from a common ancestor. They do not belong in the same taxonomic group.

The origin of the corvid songbirds presumably goes back some 90 million years to the Cretaceous when the Australian region (including New Zealand) broke away from Antarctica and drifted north. The ancestral species that gave rise to the Corvida probably reached Australia from Asia 55–60 million years ago. There was an 'adaptive radiation' of these birds into many different forms with shapes and sizes that now resemble those of their Northern Hemisphere counterparts because they move and feed in similar ways. The endemic songbird groups of the Australasian region result from adaptive radiation within the area, not from a series of invasions from Asia.

The crows, magpies and jays (corvine birds, family Corvidae) that are now such familiar, everyday birds in Asia, Europe and North America, represent an interesting twist to this story. When Australia got closer to south-east Asia, a successful crow-like species must have crossed the gap from Australia and spread far and wide to give rise to the Northern Hemisphere corvines — the new evidence suggests that these birds have Australian ancestry. We are so used to the idea that animals spread from the north to our remote part of the world that the reverse process seems surprising.

All of New Zealand's endemic songbirds are corvids except for the fernbirds (*Bowdleria*) which are passerids of the Old World warbler family. The Pipit, Welcome Swallow and Silvereye (see Part Two) are also passerids. (An American scientist, S.L. Olson, believes that the genera *Mohoua* and *Gerygone* are passerids rather than corvids, but this point is unsettled.) All New Zealand's introduced songbirds (House Sparrows, Starlings, Blackbirds, Goldfinches and so on) are passerids except for the Australian Magpie (*Gymnorhina*) and Rook (*Corvus*).

Piopio

(Family Turnagridae)

Ornithologists have always had trouble deciding what birds are the Piopio's closest relatives and therefore to what family it belongs. The Piopio has a striking superficial similarity to an Australian bowerbird, the Tooth-billed Catbird (*Ailuroedus dentirostris*), which lives in upland rainforest of north Queensland. The bowerbirds (family Ptilonorhynchidae) are rather crow-like birds with stout bills and strong feet, restricted to New Guinea and Australia. Other possibilities are that the Piopio is a bird-of-paradise (family Paradisaeidae) or a member of the whistler family (Pachycephalidae) like the Yellowhead and allies. New Zealand ornithologists have usually put it in its own family, the Turnagridae, and this has been confirmed by DNA studies. These studies showed that the Piopio is most closely related to bowerbirds, and that the ancestral Piopio may have spread to New Zealand and diverged from the bowerbird stock about 27 million years ago. The Piopio belongs with the lyrebirds and bowerbirds in a subgroup of corvids known as the Menuroidea.

Piopio

Turnagra capensis (Sparrman, 1787)

[Extinct]

The Piopio is also called the New Zealand Thrush because it superficially resembles the thrushes of Europe, but the two are not closely related. The Piopio was about the size of a Tui, and probably weighed about 100 g. The bill was stout and there were bristle-like feathers at the gape. At the time of European settlement the Piopio was widespread, and in many areas common, in forest throughout the North and South Islands. It was also found on Stephens Island in Cook Strait and there is a subfossil record from Stewart Island where the bird was not recorded historically. The last record of the North Island race was of a bird shot at Ohura in 1902. During the goldrush in Westland the Piopio was a common bird in the miners' camps, but was in decline by 1870. It was probably extinct in the South Island, as in the North, by about 1900. There have been numerous reported sightings, in both main islands, as recently as the 1960s but none has been confirmed. Early reports indicate that the Piopio lived in forest and scrub from the coast to the mountains. It ate both invertebrates and plant matter (seeds, berries) and often fed on the ground, hopping about like a Blackbird. Piopios were confiding birds that took scraps of food at camp sites in the bush. The nest was built at any height in the forest from as low as about a metre above ground. The clutch size was often two, the eggs white with brown blotches and approximately 35 mm by 25 mm. The Piopio's calls were described as 'plaintive' or 'piping', and in Buller's opinion this was the best native songster. The Piopio received the Latinised name *capensis* because there was confusion with labels, and Sparrman, who described the species in 1787 from specimens collected on Cook's second voyage, thought that the bird was from the Cape of Good Hope.

Piopio.

Pardalotes, Acanthizid Warblers and Allies
(Family Pardalotidae)

Studies of molecular biology have shown that the acanthizid warblers (formerly in a family of their own, Acanthizidae) and the pardalotes, two groups hitherto thought not to be especially closely related, belong together in the same family. Both are small birds with small, insectivorous bills. The acanthizid warblers build enclosed, hanging nests. They are largely Australian and New Guinean, with a few species extending into south-east Asia. The New Zealand representatives are two species of *Gerygone*. The pardalotes form feeding flocks outside the breeding season. The nest is typically a chamber at the end of a tunnel excavated in an earth bank or the like. Pardalotes are found in Australia, including Tasmania.

The Grey Warbler's hanging nest is thickly lined with feathers.

Grey Warbler.

Grey Warbler

(Riroriro)

Gerygone igata (Quoy and Gaimard, 1830)

This tiny bird rivals the Rifleman for small size. They weigh about the same, but the Grey Warbler is longer because the Rifleman has a reduced tail. The Grey Warbler is one of the commonest and most widely distributed New Zealand songbirds, found throughout the country wherever there are a few trees or bushes. Because of their lightness, Grey Warblers are able to hover momentarily in flight to seize insects and spiders at the ends of leaves and twigs where other birds cannot reach. They are the only mainland bird that builds an enclosed suspended nest. The nest is pear-shaped, with a small circular entrance at the side, and is usually constructed to hang from fine stems or twigs. The eggs of the clutch are laid at two-day intervals, rather than daily, which is unusual among songbirds in general, but seems to be a characteristic of the *Gerygone* and *Acanthiza* warblers and their relatives. The egg (1.5 g) is very large relative to the female's weight (6.5 g). The ratio is 23 percent — the same as in Little Spotted Kiwis, which are widely held to have the heaviest egg relative to female weight. The kiwi lays one egg while the warbler typically lays four in the space of seven days! Grey Warblers are parasitised by the Shining Cuckoo (p. 170).

A Grey Warbler at its nest.

Only the female Grey Warbler incubates the eggs, but the male assists in feeding the chicks.

Chatham Island Warbler

Gerygone albofrontata G.R. Gray, 1844
[Outlying islands only]

This larger relative of the Grey Warbler has not adapted as well as its mainland counterpart to modified habitats, and has disappeared from the northern half of Chatham Island. Other than this it is found in native forest and scrub throughout the Chatham group. Like the Grey Warbler it builds a covered hanging nest with an entrance at the side, and lays eggs at two-day intervals. It too is a host of the Shining Cuckoo. The sexes of the Chatham Island Warbler differ slightly in size and colour, the male being larger with bolder markings, unlike the Grey Warbler where the male and female are alike.

Honeyeaters
(Family Meliphagidae)

Honeyeaters are important and distinctive songbirds of the Australasian region. There are about 170 species found in Australia, New Guinea, Indonesia, New Zealand, Hawaii and islands of the southwest Pacific. Honeyeaters eat insects, fruit and nectar, and play an important ecological role by pollinating flowers and dispersing small seeds. For lapping nectar they have brush-tipped tongues that they can extend deeply into flowers. The tongue can be thrust into a flower many times per second and nectar is drawn by capillary action onto the frayed portions of the tongue. The male is larger in all three New Zealand honeyeaters.

Stitchbird

(Hihi)
Notiomystis cincta (Du Bus, 1839)

Stitchbirds are the only living honeyeaters that nest in tree-holes. It seems that another honeyeater, the extinct Kauai 'O'o (*Moho braccatus*) of Hawaii, shared this habit. Male Stitchbirds have white 'ear patches' and these tufts of feathers can be erected during behavioural interactions. This bird, or its sub-

A male Stitchbird.

Passerine Birds 121

Above: Stitchbirds feed on nectar and fruit. They take insects when feeding chicks.

Left: A female Stitchbird.

fossil bones, have been found only in the North Island. Stitchbirds were common in many parts until the early 1870s. Then they declined and by 1885 were restricted to Little Barrier Island where they persisted, and from where they are now being transferred to other islands. Not all transfers have been successful. Stitchbirds may require a greater variety of nectar- and fruit-producing plants than small islands can provide, and the more aggressive Tuis and Bellbirds may displace Stitchbirds from favoured feeding sites.

A male Bellbird.

Bellbird

(Korimako)
Anthornis melanura (Sparrman, 1786)

Bellbirds weigh slightly less than Stitchbirds, though they are a little longer. In males, one of the leading wing feathers is notched. This produces a whirring sound as they fly about during territorial encounters. Like the Tui, Bellbirds have loud musical songs. However, the bell notes they are named for sound their finest at dawn and dusk, and when given by many birds together in areas where few other species are singing. Bellbirds are found throughout much of New Zealand but they are absent from the Auckland area, Northland and most of Canterbury. Those on the Auckland Islands, with a population of Tuis, are the southernmost honeyeaters. A subspecies of Bellbird on the Chatham Islands was slightly larger than mainland birds and had some minor differences in plumage. In the 1870s it was present throughout the Chatham group and the song was said to be even richer than on the mainland. The last birds were seen on Little Mangere Island in 1906 and the population is now extinct.

Passerine Birds 123

Above: The female Bellbird has a white stripe across her cheek. Chicks are fed by both parents.

Above right: Male Bellbird.

Bellbird bathing.

Tui

Prosthemadera novaeseelandiae (Gmelin, 1788)

The Tui is the biggest New Zealand honeyeater, and the second largest surviving native songbird after the Kokako. The adults are unusual among honeyeaters in having dark iridescent plumage and tufted white feathers at the throat. A picture of a Tui in P. Brown's *New Illustrations of Zoology* (1776) was the first published illustration of a New Zealand bird. As well as a wide distribution throughout mainland New Zealand, the Tui occurs on the subtropical Kermadec Islands, subantarctic Auckland Islands and on the Chatham Islands where the birds are slightly larger and the population forms a subspecies of its own.

Above: Tui.

Left: Tui pair at nest.

Passerine Birds 125

Above: Like the Bellbird and the Stitchbird, the Tui has a brush-tipped tongue to assist with nectar feeding.

Left: Kowhai flowers provide abundant nectar for Tuis in early spring.

Australo-Papuan Robins
(Family Petroicidae)

This group of about 40 species is centred in Australia and New Guinea, with a few species in New Zealand and on islands of the south-west Pacific. Most have large heads, rounded bodies, contrasting (often brightly coloured) underparts, and an upright stance. Many have long rictal bristles at the base of their stout bill, and feed by pouncing on prey from an elevated perch. The name robin was applied by homesick settlers because of superficial similarities to the robins of Europe. The two groups are not closely related.

New Zealand Tomtit

Petroica macrocephala (Gmelin, 1789)

This small insectivore is found in bush and scrub throughout New Zealand and on the Chatham, Snares and Auckland Islands. Five subspecies are recognised. Males of the South Island race (Maori name Ngiru-ngiru) have a smudge of yellow on the breast, unlike the black and white males of the North Island race (Maori name Miromiro). The Snares Island race is all black. All except the last have a white 'frontal spot' immediately above the base of the beak. This spot they flare during encounters

Male South Island Tomtit.

Passerine Birds

A male North Island Tomtit at its nest.

Below: An immature female New Zealand Tomtit.

Female New Zealand Tomtit.

with other species of birds and with humans. The Tomtit's special mode of feeding involves scanning the understorey from a perch and then flying to the ground or another perch to seize their prey.

New Zealand's Unique Birds

Below: New Zealand Robins feed on insects and their larvae, spiders and earthworms. They sometimes eat small fruits.

A New Zealand Robin at its nest.

Right: South Island Robins often show a faint yellow colouring on the breast.

Below right: New Zealand Robin.

New Zealand Robin

(Toutouwai)

Petroica australis (Sparrman, 1788)

This is the largest of New Zealand's small native insectivorous songbirds and the largest member of the genus *Petroica*. They are found in many of the remaining larger tracts of native forest, in older pine forests and in scrub in certain areas. New Zealand Robins largely feed on the forest floor where they hop about and often tremble a foot to flush out invertebrate prey. They cache surplus food in a crevice and retrieve it later. Robins have declined, and are probably still declining, as a result of loss of habitat and predation by introduced mammals. Their habit of feeding on the ground and building their nest close to the main trunk or branches of a tree makes them especially vulnerable to predators. Their reaction time is very fast, but they can be surprised by a predator while feeding on the ground in dense cover. In some places robins are

Left and below: The Black Robin was saved from extinction when only five birds survived.

bold and inquisitive, and they will approach a quiet observer, even perching on a foot or rucksack while they scan the nearby leaf-litter for disturbed prey. Their 'inquisitiveness' is for the insects that large animals (such as people and cattle) flush as they move along. They probably followed moas in the same way. Robins flash their white 'frontal spot' in the same way as Tomtits.

Black Robin

Petroica traversi (Buller, 1872)
[Outlying islands only]

The Black Robin is the famous bird that was brought back from the brink of extinction — one of the world's conservation success stories. It was once found throughout the Chatham group, but by 1937 was restricted to tiny Little Mangere Island. Management by the Wildlife Service (now Department of Conservation) began in 1976. The entire remaining population of five males and two females was transferred to Mangere Island, where the habitat was better, and breeding productivity was increased by fostering eggs and nestlings to nests of Tomtits. The population dropped to a low of five birds (including just one female named Old Blue), but has now increased to 150–200 birds in self-maintaining populations on Mangere and South East Islands. Black Robins are entirely black as their name suggests, an example of the tendency of New Zealand birds to become dull-plumaged or even completely melanistic during their evolution in relative isolation. Named after Henry Travers (see Stephens Island Wren).

Whistlers and Allies
(Family Pachycephalidae)

This family contains about 30 species in south-east Asia, New Guinea, Australia, New Zealand and islands of the south-west Pacific. They are small but robust, predominantly insectivorous bush birds with short, stout bills and large, rounded heads. The three New Zealand species are all in the genus *Mohoua*. An American researcher (S.L. Olson) has stated that these do not belong in the Pachycephalidae, but he has not said where they do belong. The species of *Mohoua* are unusual among New Zealand birds in having evolved very distinctly different North and South Island representatives. The males are larger and heavier than females. The pelvis and hindlimbs are specialised for the use of the feet in shifting vegetation and leaf-litter while foraging. Yellowheads scratch vigorously to search through leaf-litter accumulated in forks of trees. They are the most derived with regard to their pelvic structure; Brown Creepers are the most primitive in this respect. The three species of *Mohoua* are gregarious birds, usually found in family groups or larger noisy flocks. They are insectivores that occasionally take small fruits and berries, and they will hang upside down in their search for food. All are parasitised by the Long-tailed Cuckoo (see p. 106). The species of *Mohoua* often breed communally, which is the case when pairs raise chicks assisted by non-breeding birds, usually their young from previous years. Whiteheads breed communally where their densities are high and there is little chance for young to establish their own territories.

Only the female Whitehead incubates the eggs.

Whiteheads are insectivorous.

Passerine Birds

Whitehead

(Popokatea)
Mohoua albicilla (Lesson, 1830)

Unique to the North Island, Whiteheads died out in most northern areas but persist in central and southern parts, mainly in the larger tracts of heavier bush. They also range into older pine forests and are among the commonest birds on Little Barrier and Kapiti Islands.

Above: Male Whiteheads assist in feeding the chicks. Offspring from previous broods may also feed the chicks.

Above right and centre: Yellowheads inhabit South Island beech forests. Their numbers have been considerably reduced by stoat predation.

Right: Yellowheads build a nest similar to the Whitehead's, but it is always in a crevice or a hole in a tree.

Yellowhead

(Mohua)
Mohoua ochrocephala (Gmelin, 1789)

Yellowheads were once widespread on the South Island and Stewart Island, but are now reduced to populations in a few areas, most notably Fiordland and in the Arthur's Pass area. They are the largest of the three species of *Mohoua*. By pressing the tail against trunks and branches while searching for hidden insects and spiders, Yellowheads often wear off the ends of the tail feathers to leave the spine-like shafts. The spiny tail may in turn help to support the Yellowhead in certain foraging positions. Yellowheads nest in holes, unlike their two congeners, but unusually for a hole-nester they build a cup-shaped nest, not an enclosed one.

Brown Creeper.

Brown Creeper

(Pipipi)

Mohoua novaeseelandiae (Gmelin, 1789)

The smallest *Mohoua*, the Brown Creeper is restricted to South and Stewart Islands, like the Yellowhead. They are at home in scrub as well as forest, including subalpine scrub at the treeline. They may have arisen as an alpine derivative of the Yellowhead, that subsequently reinvaded lowland habitats and came to overlap the Yellowhead in distribution.

The insectivorous Brown Creeper is common in forest or scrub throughout the South Island. It is absent from the North Island.

New Zealand Wattlebirds

(Family Callaeidae)

This family of three species is unique to New Zealand. They may be closely related to the starlings (family Sturnidae), which the Saddleback and male Huia resemble in head shape, or they may be close to the Piopio (family Turnagridae, in turn close to the bowerbirds). They are not related to the Australian wattlebirds, which are honeyeaters. New Zealand wattlebirds get their name from the pair of coloured fleshy wattles at the gape, one on each side. The wattles are smallest in juveniles and largest in adult males, so they probably help to communicate the age and breeding status of individuals. Their wings are short and rounded and they fly weakly, but the legs are very powerful with strong claws, which suit these birds for a largely tree-dwelling existence in the deep forest. They use their strong bills to probe for food, especially large insects in decaying wood.

North Island Kokako.

A Kokako feeding chicks with green scale insects. Although the Kokako diet consists mainly of fruits, flowers and vegetation, insect food is given to the chicks to provide extra protein.

Kokako

Callaeas cinerea (Gmelin, 1788)

The Kokako is the largest surviving native songbird, with a weight of about 230 g. It has large, strong legs and hops and leaps about the forest with great agility, but the wings are reduced and the flight is weak. Its beautiful song contains rich organ-like notes. Kokakos are largely vegetarian, unlike the other two New Zealand wattlebirds which are largely insectivorous. They eat leaves all year, fruits and berries when available, and forest invertebrates, particularly in summer when raising young. They suffer from predation by introduced mammals, and also from competition for food with the introduced Brush-tailed Possum (*Trichosurus vulpecula*). Kokakos build a large cup-shaped nest. At the time of European settlement they were present in forests throughout North, South and Stewart Islands. They were once even more widespread, for their bones are numerous in certain areas, such as sand-dunes of Northland, which did not provide suitable habitat when European settlement began. This is evidence of the deleterious effect that Maori settlement had on the New Zealand avifauna. The North Island subspecies (Blue-wattled Crow) has blue wattles (pink in the juvenile). It has declined to a few remnant populations in forests of the northern half of the island, and has been successfully transferred to Little Barrier and Kapiti Islands. The South Island subspecies (Orange-wattled Crow) has orange wattles but appears to be extinct. There have been recent unconfirmed reports of this bird but it has not been reliably recorded since around the mid-1990s.

Top: A male Kokako offers a berry to the female during courtship.

Above: Kokako usually sing only at dawn.

A male North Island Saddleback.

Saddleback

(Tieke)

Philesturnus carunculatus (Gmelin, 1789)

Saddlebacks are the least specialised of the New Zealand wattlebirds. They eat invertebrates, fruits and nectar. Their jaw structure is like that of Starlings (*Sturnus vulgaris*) which allows forceful gaping — using the opening action of the beak to prise open pieces of bark and gain entry to crevices where prey are found. Saddlebacks nest in tree-holes, rock clefts or dense tangles of vegetation, usually near the ground — they do not have an open, cup-nest like the Kokako. The North and South Island populations of the Saddleback are separate subspecies. The adults are similar but the juveniles are very different. North Island juveniles are like the adult (black with a chestnut saddle), but South Island juveniles are chocolate brown all over. Like Kokakos, Saddlebacks were present in forests throughout North, South and Stewart Islands at the time of European settlement. They were also present (unlike Kokakos) on many offshore islands. By about 1950 they were reduced to Hen Island in the north and three islands off Stewart Island. Pioneering transfers by staff of the New Zealand Wildlife Service (now the Department of Conservation) established the species on several other islands, bringing it back from the brink of extinction — one of New Zealand's earliest conservation successes.

New Zealand's **Unique Birds**

Left: The wattle of this immature Saddleback is not fully developed.

Below: The female Saddleback is responsible for incubation. The male feeds her at 50- to 70-minute intervals. Both parents feed the chicks with insects.

The Saddleback often holds its food in one foot, parrot fashion.

Huia

Heteralocha acutirostris (Gould, 1837)
[Extinct]

The Huia was about the size of an Australian Magpie (*Gymnorhina tibicen*) and probably weighed about 300 g. The bill of the male and female are the most radically different in shape of any bird. The female's bill is much longer (average 96 mm) and therefore more curved than the male's (average 60 mm). The Latinised name *Heteralocha* means 'different spouse', referring to the sexual dimorphism. The bill differences suggest that the sexes were specialised for feeding in very different ways. Naturalists who watched Huias feeding recorded that the male tended to chisel at the outer surfaces of decaying or live wood, whereas the female was able to probe deeply into soft wood or crevices to retrieve insects unobtainable to the male. Pairs seemed to co-operate in their search for food, the diet comprising insects, spiders and berries. Recent study of the anatomy of the Huia's head and neck has shown that the male had a capacity for forceful gaping — inserting his bill into rotting wood and forcing his beak open to split the wood. Subfossil bones of the Huia have been found only in the North Island, at cave and dune sites from North Cape to the Wellington area. However, during the period of European settlement Huias were recorded only in the southern part of the island — from the Raukumara Range and Turakina River south to Wellington. This suggests that the species declined between the arrival of Polynesians in New Zealand and the arrival of Europeans. Maori probably ate Huias and certainly prized their beaks and tail feathers for ornamentation. The first published reference to the Huia was in the Reverend William Yate's *Account of New Zealand* (1835), which was rather late given that many New Zealand birds were collected on Cook's voyages. The male and female Huias were described and named as separate species in 1837, an error which became apparent later. There have been no reliable sightings of the Huia since W.W. Smith saw three in the Tararua Ranges on 28 December 1907. The writings of New Zealand naturalists of the late nineteenth century indicate that the Huia kept to the depths of the forest, moving about mainly on foot whether on the ground or in the canopy, and flying weakly. The name 'huia' is thought to be an onomatopoeic rendition of the alarm call, which was a shrill whistle. Little is known about the Huia's breeding. The saucer-shaped nest was large, as expected for so large a bird — about 35 cm across with a smaller depression lined with fine material for the eggs. The breeding season was early summer when most forest birds breed. Two to four eggs were laid, each about 45 mm by 30 mm, and greyish with brown and purplish markings. Towards the end of the nineteenth century the Huia was one of New Zealand's best-known birds internationally, and natural history museums and private collectors throughout the world sought to purchase mounted specimens for display. Collectors with hunting rifles were probably a significant factor in finishing off so tame a bird at a time when it was already declining as a result of habitat clearance and the effect of introduced predators. Regulations of February 1892 made it illegal to kill or take Huias in any part of New Zealand, but enforcement was another matter. Legend has it that when the Duke of York (later King George V) visited Rotorua in 1902, a Maori guide gave him a Huia's tail feather which he wore in his hatband, creating an immediate craze which pushed the price of the feathers to one pound each. Each Huia had twelve tail feathers, as is typical of most songbirds. The feathers were traded by jewellers and second-hand dealers as late as the 1930s. In 1921 G.E. Mason published a report on five ticks which he found attached to one of the wattles of a Huia collected near Masterton in 1883. The ticks belonged to two species present in India and it has been surmised that they travelled to New Zealand with Common Mynas (*Acridotheres tristis*) which were introduced from India in 1875. The ticks may have transmitted a disease to Huias.

Study skins of the Huia showing female (above) and male (below).

Crows
(Family Corvidae)

Crows are large, predominantly black songbirds with stout beaks and robust legs. They are adaptable, intelligent and omnivorous. The cawing of crows is a familiar sound almost everywhere in the world except New Zealand, which has no living representatives of this family except the introduced and localised Rook (*Corvus frugilegus*). Because they are so widespread and common around the world it comes as no surprise to find that until relatively recently New Zealand had its own crow.

New Zealand Crow
Palaeocorax moriorum (Forbes, 1892)
[Extinct]

This is the largest New Zealand passerine bird, and its weight has been estimated at 0.9–1.0 kg. Subfossil bones of the New Zealand Crow have been found at both natural sites and in Maori (or Moriori) kitchen middens on the North and South Islands and on the Chatham Islands. There is also one record from Stewart Island. The first bones were found on the Chathams by H.O. Forbes who described the species (and the genus) in 1892. It probably fed on both invertebrate animals and plant foods, especially seeds and berries. Most records are from coastal sites, and the scarcity of its remains in cave sites, most of which are inland, suggests that it was a bird of the coastal lowlands.

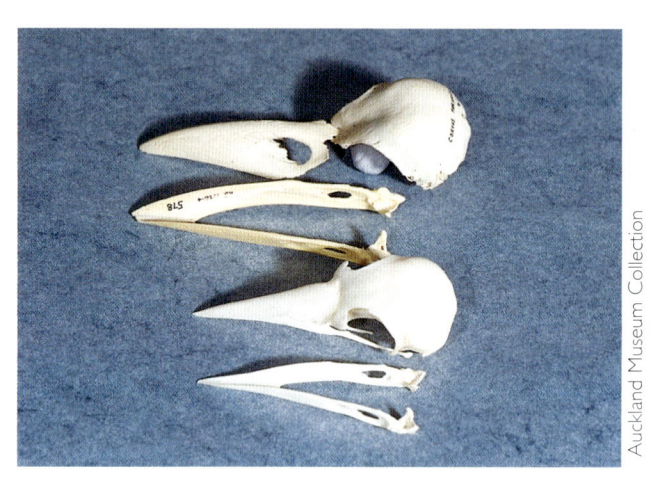

Skull and mandibles of the New Zealand Crow (at rear), with those of the Australian Magpie (at front) for comparison.

Old World Warblers
(Family Sylviidae)

The members of this large family of small songbirds, mainly restricted to the Old World, have fine-pointed bills for catching insects. Most are drab in colour, especially in temperate areas. They are passerid songbirds that have successfully invaded the Australasian region, despite the presence of the native corvid songbirds. The fernbirds are closely related to the grassbirds (*Megalurus*) of Australia. Other representatives of the family in Australia are the reed-warblers and songlarks. In New Zealand the two species of fernbirds are the only endemic passerid songbirds. Fernbirds are about the size of

House Sparrows. They have long tails, the feathers of which are degenerate with a loose, spiky appearance. Fernbirds have a strangely shaped pelvis and robust leg bones. These appear to be adaptations to the use of the legs in foraging and locomotion, for fernbirds shift leaf-litter with their feet, and they perch astride reeds and other flimsy foliage which requires greater gymnastic ability than perching on a solid branch.

Fernbird

(Matata)
Bowdleria punctata (Quoy and Gaimard, 1830)
Fernbirds once occurred throughout New Zealand in swampland, fernland and scrubland, but are now much reduced in range on the mainland. There are separate North, South and Stewart Island subspecies, and two further subspecies occur on Codfish Island (off Stewart Island) and the Snares Islands (south of Stewart). Fernbirds usually keep to low, dense vegetation. They are weak fliers and fly reluctantly, when forced from cover, with the tail hanging down.

North Island Fernbird.

Unlike many members of the family, Fernbirds lack a loud, musical song. They keep contact in dense cover with short, metallic-sounding calls. One distinctive call ('u-tick') is given by the male alone or by a duetting pair, the male sounding 'u' and the female responding instantaneously with the 'tick'. Fernbirds are strongly territorial. The nestling has three dark spots on its bright yellow tongue, two at the back and one at the tip. These signal the parents when they feed the chicks, and such mouth markings are characteristic of the family Sylviidae.

A Fernbird with a spider. Note the 'fern-like' tail with disjointed barbs.

Above: A Fernbird and nest. Both parents feed the chicks with insects and spiders.

Above right: Chatham Island Fernbird.

Chatham Island Fernbird

Bowdleria rufescens (Buller, 1869)
[Extinct. Outlying islands only]

In the Chatham Island Fernbird the throat and breast are white without conspicuous spots, and the upper parts are reddish-brown. In the mainland Fernbird the throat and breast are heavily spotted and the upper parts brownish. In 1868 Charles Traill discovered this species on Mangere Island in the Chatham group. He saw a small bird in the undergrowth and killed it with a stone. Walter Buller examined the specimen and described it as new in 1869. Fernbirds were also recorded on Pitt Island where burning and introduced cats may have been factors in their demise. Bones have been found in subfossil sites, including kitchen middens, and these establish the former occurrence of the species on Chatham Island itself. The last museum specimen was shot on Mangere Island by one of Lord Rothschild's collectors. The species has been extinct since about 1900. The Chatham Island Fernbird presumably had habits much like its mainland relative.

Part Two
Other Native Birds

Top: Grey Duck and ducklings. Sexes are similar in appearance.

Above: The Australasian Shoveler drake is brightly coloured, with the female being drab-coloured.

This section is a brief overview of the native New Zealand birds other than the endemic species already covered. The birds mentioned here are found naturally in New Zealand and are therefore native New Zealand birds, but the species to which they belong also occur elsewhere and are therefore not unique to New Zealand. Some are endemic at the level of the subspecies (see Table Four, p. 182), indicating that they are weakly distinguishable as New Zealand forms. Others are not significantly different from populations overseas. In fact, several of our commonest and best-known native birds are Australian species that established and spread within the last 40–140 years. Previously they were known in New Zealand only as stragglers.

The number of endemic subspecies (Table Four) is a little unstable — what are listed one day as subspecies may later come to be regarded as full species, or vice versa (see Species-level Endemics, p. 13). The enumeration is also rather arbitrary — some birds narrowly miss out on being subspecies endemic to New Zealand, such as the Grey Duck, *Anas superciliosa superciliosa*, because there is a population on Macquarie Island, and the Shining Cuckoo, *Chrysococcyx lucidus lucidus*, because it breeds on Norfolk Island.

Only the most common or notable of the native birds are mentioned by name in this section, with the emphasis on mainland species rather than those that reach their greatest abundance on the outlying islands. There are many less common natives. These include rare stragglers and vagrants, especially various species of migratory seabirds and waders which are seen occasionally, or certain Australian birds very rarely blown across the Tasman Sea. These are all natives so long as they arrive unassisted.

Swans, Geese and Ducks
(Family Anatidae)

New Zealand's lakes, ponds, swamps and estuaries support a good variety of waterfowl. The **Grey Duck** (Parera) *Anas superciliosa,* is common, but now found mainly in wilder areas. It is uncommon in farmed areas and on city lakes, where it has suffered from competition and hybridisation with the introduced Mallard, *A. platyrhynchos*. The **Australasian Shoveler** (Kuruwhengi) *A. rhynchotis,* is a widespread native duck, and an endemic subspecies. The males in breeding plumage are particularly handsome. One of the smallest New Zealand ducks is the **Grey Teal** (Tete) *A. gracilis*, common throughout much of the country. It was rare and local until the 1950s, when it increased dramatically with influxes from Australia.

Grey Teal feed by filtering the surface water of shallow lagoons.

Above: Great Crested Grebes inhabit subalpine lakes of the South Island.

Right: A Great Crested Grebe at its nest, composed of sticks and waterweed. Incubation is shared by both sexes.

Grebes
(Family Podicipedidae)

The **Great Crested Grebe** (Puteketeke) *Podiceps cristatus,* lives on the large inland lakes of the South Island, where it is uncommon. It is absent from the North Island, but is remarkable for its wide distribution in other regions, including Europe, much of Asia, sub-Saharan Africa and Australia.

Penguins
(Family Spheniscidae)

The **Blue Penguin** (Korora) *Eudyptula minor*, the smallest of the world's penguins, is common around the New Zealand coast. They are often seen swimming in coastal waters. When they come ashore at night to breed they can be very noisy. Blue Penguins are also found in southern Australia, where they are called Fairy Penguins. One or more subspecies are endemic to New Zealand — the number has not been settled.

The Blue Penguin is commonly seen around New Zealand's sheltered coasts.

Shearwaters, Fulmars, Prions and Petrels

(Family Procellariidae)

New Zealand has a great diversity of these seabirds. They feed at sea, and because of introduced mammalian predators they now breed mostly on inaccessible islands and headlands. They therefore make little visible impact though they are one of the dominant elements in the avifauna.

Top: The Sooty Shearwater is the commonest shearwater, and millions nest in burrows on many islands of southern New Zealand. The developed chicks, known as 'muttonbirds', are legally taken as traditional Maori food.

Above: A Flesh-footed Shearwater.

Shearwaters, Fulmars, Prions and Petrels

Among the shearwaters, the **Flesh-footed Shearwater** *Puffinus carneipes*, **Sooty Shearwater** (Titi) *P. griseus*, and **Little Shearwater** *P. assimilis*, are common in coastal waters. Many millions of Sooty Shearwaters breed on islands and headlands throughout the New Zealand region. They are one of the main muttonbirds and about a quarter of a million fat chicks are harvested annually by Maori in the Stewart Island area. The Little Shearwater has two endemic subspecies in the New Zealand region.

Above left: A Broad-billed Prion *Pachyptila vittata*, one of six species of prions commonly seen around the southern New Zealand coast.

Above: A Flesh-footed Shearwater

Left: The Little or Allied Shearwater is the smallest of the shearwaters.

Shearwaters, Fulmars, Prions and Petrels

The Giant Petrel is the largest member of the petrel family. It is a scavenger but also feeds on live squid.

Top: A Cape Pigeon, or Pintado Petrel. Its mottled black and white markings are unusual for a seabird.

Above: The large Grey-faced Petrel nests on many mainland headlands, as well as offshore islands of northern New Zealand.

The **Common Diving Petrel** (Kuaka) *Pelecanoides urinatrix,* is a small, plump seabird that breeds all around the subantarctic zone and in some adjacent areas. It nests abundantly on offshore and outlying islands of the New Zealand region. Diving petrels are auk-like in their ability to dive and swim under water. The **Cape Pigeon** *Daption capense,* with its spectacular black and white speckled plumage, is unusually striking for a seabird. It ranges throughout the southern oceans where it breeds on islands and the Antarctic coast. An endemic subspecies breeds in the New Zealand area, and both this and a second subspecies are common in waters off the North and South Islands, especially in winter.

The largest members of the family are the giant petrels. They are the only tube-nosed seabirds that forage on land (to scavenge dead seals and penguins) and they walk well. The **Northern Giant Petrel** *Macronectes halli*, breeds on islands off Stewart Island, on the Chathams and on various subantarctic islands in the New Zealand sector and beyond. It is commonly seen in New Zealand waters, especially in Cook Strait. The **Fairy Prion** (Titi Wainui) *Pachyptila turtur,* is the commonest of six species of prions that frequent the New Zealand coasts. It breeds on many islands around the New Zealand coast and is the seabird most frequently washed up dead on our beaches.

Among the gadfly petrels, two in particular need to be mentioned here. The **Black-winged Petrel** *Pterodroma nigripennis,* is a subtropical species that breeds on the Kermadecs, the Chathams and a few islands off the northern North Island. It is common at sea in the New Zealand area. An endemic subspecies of the **Grey-faced Petrel** (Oi) *Pt. macroptera,* breeds on islands and headlands of the northern North Island. There are several large colonies. The largest — on Whale Island in the Bay of Plenty — has about 35,000 pairs.

Albatrosses, Mollymawks and Storm Petrels

Albatrosses and Mollymawks
(Family Diomedeidae)

Nearly three-quarters of the world's species of albatrosses are known from the New Zealand region. Besides the endemic Royal Albatross, New Zealand has a second 'great albatross', the **Wandering Albatross** *Diomedea exulans*, with two endemic subspecies. Two of the commonest albatrosses are the **Black-browed Mollymawk** *Thalassarche melanophrys*, with one endemic subspecies in New Zealand, and the **White-capped or Shy Mollymawk** *Th. cauta*, with two. They all have a graceful, soaring flight. Many have the habit of following boats, especially fishing vessels, and large numbers have come to grief by swallowing baited hooks.

Storm Petrels
(Family Hydrobatidae)

The **White-faced Storm Petrel** (Takahikare-moana) *Pelagodroma marina*, is the commonest of several storm petrels in the New Zealand region. They are the smallest of the tube-nosed seabirds. With long, thin legs dangling, they hover or patter at the surface of waves, gliding and hopping to seize prey at the water's surface. The White-faced Storm Petrel is also called the Jesus Christ Bird because it appears to walk on water, or the Dancing Dolly.

Above left: A Shy, or White-capped, Mollymawk has longer wings than other species of mollymawks.

Above right: A tiny White-faced Storm Petrel. Storm petrels are the smallest of the tube-nosed seabirds, being smaller than the common Blackbird.

Gannets and Boobies
(Family Sulidae)

A very important large coastal bird is the **Australasian Gannet** (Takapu) *Morus serrator*, which breeds on islands around the New Zealand coast, and on a few headlands, most notably Cape Kidnappers, near Napier, and Muriwai, near Auckland. Most of the young birds migrate to south-east Australian waters and return to New Zealand at three to seven years old.

Above: Gannet numbers in New Zealand are increasing annually by over two percent. The colony at Muriwai is expanding. Both parents incubate the single egg under the web of a foot.

Left: An Australasian Gannet.

Cormorants and Shags
(Family Phalacrocoracidae)

Many of the New Zealand shags are endemic, but others belong to widely distributed species. Of the latter, the two commonest are the **Black Shag** (Kawau) *Phalacrocorax carbo,* and the **Little Shag** (Kawaupaka) *Ph. melanoleucos*. They live in sheltered coastal waters, but also far inland around lakes, streams and rivers. A less widespread species, the **Pied Shag** (Karuhiruhi) *Ph. varius*, is never far from the coast.

Right: Little Black Shags *Ph. sulcirostris*, occur mainly in the North Island. They feed in both sea and freshwater, fishing in packs. They progress across the fishing area with the rear birds 'leap frogging' to the front.

Below: The Black Shag is the largest and shyest of New Zealand's twelve shag species. Subspecies of the Black Shag are found in many countries of the world. Both parents incubate. Many kinds of fish are caught and chicks are fed by regurgitation.

Below: There are variations in the plumage of Little Shags — 'pied', 'white-throated' or 'smudgy'. The bird on the right shows the 'pied' form.

A white-throated plumage form of the Little Shag.

Herons and Bitterns
(Family Ardeidae)

Though not common in New Zealand, the **White Heron** (Kotuku) *Egretta alba*, has a special significance for its elegance and beauty. It is found worldwide in tropical and temperate regions. The commonest heron in New Zealand is now the **White-Faced Heron** *Ardea novaehollandiae*, an Australian species which was a straggler to New Zealand until 1941 when it was confirmed breeding in Otago and after which it spread to all areas. The **Reef Heron** (Matuku Moana) *Egretta sacra*, a coastal species, and the **Australasian Bittern** (Matuku) *Botaurus poiciloptilus*, frequenter of swamps, are uncommon.

Right: Reef Herons feed in marine habitats and only rarely venture inland.

Above: White-faced Herons feed at tidal estuaries, among mangroves, around freshwater lakes and streams and in pastures.

Left: These White Herons are nesting in a colony in trees on the banks of the Waitangiroto River near Okarito in South Westland. Both parents incubate and feed the chicks. During the nesting season the White Heron's bill changes colour from yellow to black.

Herons and Bitterns 155

The male Australasian Bittern takes no part in the rearing of the chicks. The female is entirely responsible for incubation and feeding. Nests are well concealed in thick stands of raupo or sedges.

Ibises and Spoonbills
(Family Threskiornithidae)

The magnificent **Royal Spoonbill** (Kotuku-ngutupapa) *Platalea regia*, with its pure white plumage and large, black, spoon-shaped bill, was an Australian straggler first confirmed breeding in 1949 at Okarito (Westland). It has steadily increased and is now locally common.

Above: Royal Spoonbills nest in loose colonies. Both parents incubate, and feed the chicks on small fish and invertebrates.

Above right: Royal Spoonbills are in a different family from herons. Unlike herons they fly with their neck extended.

Right: Royal Spoonbills build a substantial nest of sticks, on the ground or in a tree.

Hawks and Eagles
(Family Accipitridae)

The only common raptor in New Zealand is the **Australasian Harrier** (Kahu) *Circus approximans*, found in open country everywhere. As it soars and glides it holds its wings upwards in a shallow V-shape. Its distribution and numbers have been boosted by forest clearance, and also by roading, for a big part of the diet is road-killed animals, especially possums and rabbits.

The Australasian Harrier is the most common New Zealand raptor. They feed on small mammals, particularly rabbits, birds, frogs, lizards and large insects. They are often killed by traffic when scavenging carrion on roadsides.

Rails, Gallinules and Coots
(Family Rallidae)

Important native rails are the **Banded Rail** (Moho-pereru) *Gallirallus philippensis*, **Spotless Crake** (Puweto) *Porzana tabuensis*, and **Marsh Crake** (Koitareke) *P. pusilla*. All favour dense cover and are secretive, so despite being locally common they are rarely seen.

The **Pukeko** *Porhyrio porphyrio*, known elsewhere in the world as the Purple Swamphen, is abundant and well-known throughout the country. On lakes in many areas, the highly aquatic **Eurasian Coot** *Fulica atra*, has now become common. It was a rare straggler until it established and spread after 1958 when it was found breeding in Otago.

Above: A Banded Rail. This secretive bird is common in mangrove swamps which are backed by sedge-lined saltings.

Right: A Banded Rail at its nest. The bird bends the sedges over to form a bower. This hides the nest from predators such as harriers.

Rails, Gallinules and Coots

Left: Eurasian Coots reached New Zealand from Australia in the late 1950s. They are now widespread on many lakes, particularly those fringed with rushes.

Below: A Pukeko at its nest in a raupo swamp, with a newly hatched chick. Sometimes two females will lay in the same nest and may be accompanied by one or two males, all sharing incubation and feeding of the chicks. The chicks leave the nest when a few days old.

A Spotless Crake at its nest. Although quite common in freshwater swamps, the birds are very secretive and seldom venture out of thick cover. Both sexes incubate the 3–4 egg clutch and the chicks leave the nest and forage with the parents when three days old.

Sandpipers and Snipes

Thousands of waders spend the summer months in New Zealand after having nested in the tundra regions of Siberia and Alaska.

Sandpipers and Snipes
(Family Scolopacidae)

New Zealand is the destination for a portion of the world's arctic waders, many of which belong in this family. They breed in the arctic or subarctic tundra and undertake a spectacular trans-equatorial migration to spend the northern winter in the Southern Hemisphere. Those reaching New Zealand arrive between September and November, and most leave in March/April. Some — probably mostly yearlings — over-winter in New Zealand. The adults moult during the southern summer.

The arctic waders are found in our estuaries where they feed on the mudflats and in shallow water. Most have whitish underparts and darker upperparts heavily speckled in shades of brown and grey. They are sometimes seen with traces of their brighter, usually rusty red-tinged, breeding plumage.

The commonest arctic wader in New Zealand is the **Bar-tailed Godwit** (Kuaka) *Limosa lapponica*, with a summer population of 85,000–105,000. Second most common is the **Lesser Knot** (Huahou) *Calidris canutus*, with 50,000–70,000 each summer. The **Turnstone** *Arenaria interpres*, is the third most numerous arctic wader (5000–7000 in summer). The fourth commonest is the **Pacific Golden Plover** (see Charadriidae). Fifth most common is the **Red-necked Stint** *Calidris ruficollis* (150–300 birds during summer). There are many other arctic migrants that reach New Zealand but in lesser numbers.

Above: Bar-tailed Godwits.

Right: Eastern Curlews *Numenius madagascariensis*, are the largest of the migrant waders. Small numbers arrive in New Zealand in late spring.

Sandpipers and Snipes

Left: Over 50,000 Lesser Knots, a bird half the size of a godwit, arrive in New Zealand at the same time as the other migrant waders. Knots often mingle with godwits at high-tide roosts.

Centre left: Curlew Sandpipers *Calidris ferruginea*, are the commonest sandpipers among the visiting arctic waders. Before returning to their nesting grounds in Siberia, the males assume a very bright-coloured nuptial plumage.

Below left: A Wandering Tattler *Tringa incana*. A small number of these arctic waders visit New Zealand each summer.

Below: Turnstones are the third most numerous of the arctic waders to visit New Zealand. They feed by turning over small stones and shells to expose marine invertebrates.

Oystercatchers
(Family Haematopodidae)

The **South Island Pied Oystercatcher** (Torea) *Haematopus ostralegus*, breeds mainly in the inland South Island but migrates to estuaries throughout the country where it spends autumn and winter. It is one of New Zealand's most important wading birds with a total population of about 85,000.

Above: South Island Pied Oystercatchers nest on South Island riverbeds and farm pasture. Tens of thousands of birds migrate to the North Island after nesting, to spend the autumn and winter months feeding on tidal mudflats and estuaries.

Left: South Island Pied Oystercatchers are resident waders which are increasing in number.

Stilts and Avocets
(Family Recurvirostridae)

The **Pied Stilt** (Poaka) *Himantopus himantopus*, which occurs widely around the world, is common all over New Zealand on riverbeds, damp pastures, lakes and estuaries.

Above: Pied Stilts are found on coastal mudflats and estuaries, lakes, riverbeds, swamplands and wet paddocks, where they feed on a wide range of insects, molluscs, marine organisms and earthworms. They are often found in large flocks.

Left: Pied Stilts nest on shingle riverbeds, sand-dunes and pastures.

Plovers, Dotterels and Lapwings
(Family Charadriidae)

The **Spur-winged Plover** *Vanellus miles*, was a rare straggler from Australia. It began breeding in Southland in about 1932 and has reached the stage where it is common nearly everywhere in open areas. The **Pacific Golden Plover** *Pluvialis fulva*, is an arctic migrant (see Scolopacidae) with a summer population in New Zealand of 600–1200.

Above: Spur-winged Plovers successfully established in Southland in the 1930s. They have now spread throughout New Zealand, inhabiting pastures, lake shores, riverbeds and coastal areas.

Left: A Pacific Golden Plover. About 1000 visit New Zealand each summer. Apart from feeding on mudflats and saltmarshes, Pacific Golden Plovers also feed on coastal grasslands where they eat insects and earthworms.

Gulls and Terns
(Family Laridae)

The two common seagulls of New Zealand are the large **Black-backed Gull** (Karoro) *Larus dominicanus*, and the smaller **Red-billed Gull** (Tarapunga) *L. novaehollandiae*. These are the gulls regularly seen in coastal towns and cities.

The largest of several terns in New Zealand is the **Caspian Tern** (Taranui) *Sterna caspia*, which occurs almost worldwide in temperate areas. It is widely distributed in New Zealand but nowhere in large numbers. The commonest New Zealand tern is the **White-fronted Tern** (Tara) *S. striata*, found all around the coast. Most juveniles and some adults winter in southeast Australian coastal waters. This species would be a New Zealand endemic except that since 1979 some have bred on islands of Bass Strait between Victoria and Tasmania.

The White-fronted Tern is our commonest tern.

Gulls and Terns

Left: The large Black-backed Gull inhabits coastal environments, but is also found inland, sometimes at high altitudes. They nest in loose colonies, or frequently in single pairs on headlands and coastal rock stacks.

Below: Caspian Terns are the largest of the four tern species which nest in New Zealand. They nest in large colonies on secluded sandy beaches and shell banks. Some pairs nest separately on rocky coastal outcrops.

The common Red-billed Gull is found in marine habitats, but is also regularly seen around towns seeking out food scraps.

Gulls and Terns

Above: White-fronted Terns nest in colonies on sand or shelly beaches and on rocky coastal islets. Young birds migrate to spend the winter months on the south-east coast of Australia.

Above right: Pairs of the rare, diminutive Fairy Tern *Sterna nereis*, nest in isolation on a few sandy ocean beaches north of Auckland.

The incubation and feeding of Fairy Tern chicks is shared by both parents.

Parrots and Lorikeets

Above: Red-crowned Parakeets are common on many offshore islands but are uncommon in mainland forests.

Left: A Red-crowned Parakeet pair at the entrance to their nest in the cavity of a pohutukawa tree.

Parrots and Lorikeets
(Family Psittacidae)

The **Red-crowned Parakeet** (Kakariki) *Cyanoramphus novaezelandiae,* is found on New Caledonia and Norfolk Island as well as New Zealand, and was once present on Lord Howe Island. It is now rare in the North and South Islands but is common on Stewart Island and many offshore and outlying islands. There are four endemic subspecies (see Table Four) with the nominate subspecies *C. n. novaezelandiae* on North, South and Stewart Islands, and Reischek's Parakeet on the Antipodes Islands.

Cuckoos and Allies
(Family Cuculidae)

The **Shining Cuckoo** (Pipiwharauroa) *Chrysococcyx lucidus,* belongs to a group of small cuckoos with iridescent plumage. It breeds on mainland New Zealand and the Chatham Islands, where it parasitises the Grey Warbler and Chatham Island Warbler, respectively. It also breeds in south-west and south-east Australia, Vanuatu, New Caledonia and on Norfolk Island. Birds breeding in the temperate zone migrate north to spend the southern winter in the tropics between Indonesia and the Solomon Islands. New Zealand birds go to the latter, which involves a spectacular migration.

The Shining Cuckoo (left) parasitises the Grey Warbler (above), forcing its host to incubate its egg and feed its chick. Shining Cuckoos migrate between the Solomon Islands and New Zealand.

Typical Owls

Left: Moreporks feed mainly on insects, but also take small birds, geckos and rodents.

Below left: The Morepork is New Zealand's only surviving native owl. The Little Owl *Athene noctua*, found only in the South Island, was introduced from Europe.

Below: Moreporks nest in holes in trees or in clumps of perching epiphytes. When chicks are about two-and-a-half weeks old they often leave the nest cavity to await the arrival of their parents bringing food.

Typical Owls
(Family Strigidae)

The **Morepork** (Ruru) *Ninox novaeseelandiae,* is a native owl common throughout New Zealand in wooded areas including suburbs. It roosts by day in dense vegetation, and is active at night. The haunting call ('more-pork') is distinctive. The same species once occurred on Lord Howe Island (extinct) and persists on Norfolk Island. A similar (sometimes considered the same) species is found in Australia.

Forest Kingfishers
(Family Halcyonidae)

The **New Zealand Kingfisher** (Kotare) *Todiramphus sanctus,* is locally common and the same species is present in Australia and New Caledonia, with migrants from Australia reaching south-east Asia and New Guinea. They have wide habitat preferences — in New Zealand they can feed on tidal mudflats, in farmed areas, along riverbanks, and at the edge or in the canopy of forests. In winter, many high-altitude and forest-dwelling kingfishers migrate to lowland sites.

Above: The New Zealand Kingfisher is found in a wide range of habitats: on sheltered coasts, in open country, near lakes and in forests.

Far left: New Zealand Kingfishers nest in holes they bore in dead trees or in clay banks.

Left: A New Zealand Kingfisher diving for a fish. The birds feed on insects, earthworms, small fish and lizards, sometimes also taking small birds and mice.

Fantails and Allies

Above: **A New Zealand Fantail at its nest. Both parents incubate and feed the chicks on insects and spiders. This photograph shows a late season nest. The tail feathers of the parent are worn.**

Left: **These New Zealand Fantail chicks are almost ready to fledge.**

Fantails and Allies
(Family Dicruridae)

One of the commonest and best-loved New Zealand songbirds is the **New Zealand (or Grey) Fantail** (Piwakawaka) *Rhipidura fuliginosa*. It lives throughout the country with endemic subspecies inhabiting the North, South and Chatham Islands. The same species occurs in Australia and on nearby islands such as New Caledonia and the Solomons. A black colour form is present in New Zealand, being much more common in the southern race than in the northern.

Wagtails and Pipits

The New Zealand Pipit is found in rough grassland, coastal sand-dunes and in subalpine herbfields.

New Zealand Pipit. Nests are built among rough herbage and on grass-covered banks. Built on the ground, they are subject to predation by Australian Magpies *Gymnorhina tibicen*, and by rats.

Wagtails and Pipits
(Family Motacillidae)

The species of pipit called *Anthus novaeseelandiae* is widespread in Africa, much of Eurasia, Indonesia and Australasia. New Zealand has four endemic subspecies which inhabit open but uncultivated areas such as sand-dunes and subalpine herbfields. They are locally common on the main islands (the nominate race), and on the Chatham (*chathamensis*), Antipodes (*steindachneri*) and Auckland and Campbell Islands (*aucklandicus*). Biochemical studies have suggested that the island forms may be species in their own right.

Swallows and Martins
(Family Hirundinidae)

The **Welcome Swallow** *Hirundo tahitica,* is a recent colonist from Australia. It was a rare straggler until 1958 when breeding was recorded for the first time in Northland. Now they are abundant in open country throughout New Zealand. The mud nest is attached to bridges, culverts, houses, sheds, jetties and the like.

Above: Welcome Swallows bred successfully in northern New Zealand in 1958. They are now common throughout New Zealand in open country and on coasts.

Left: Welcome Swallow. Both parents share incubation and feed the chicks with insects caught in flight.

White-eyes

(Family Zosteropidae)

The commonest native song-bird is probably the **Silvereye** (Tauhou) *Zosterops lateralis*. It apparently became established after an influx of these birds from Australia in 1856. Before then it was a rare straggler but it is now found everywhere and is well known in gardens.

Above: The Silvereye is our commonest songbird. They are found in forest, scrub and suburban gardens and are often seen searching for insects among mangroves. They feed on a variety of insects, spiders and fruit.

Left: Silvereye. Both parents share incubation and feeding of the chicks, with up to three broods raised each year.

Table One

The 37 Genera of Birds Endemic to New Zealand

Extinct genera are marked [E]. The table shows the classification of the birds into orders and families. See Table Two for the common names.

Order STRUTHIONIFORMES
Family Emeidae
    Anomalopteryx [E]
    Megalapteryx [E]
    Pachyornis [E]
    Emeus [E]
    Euryapteryx [E]
Family Dinornithidae
    Dinornis [E]
Family Apterygidae
    Apteryx

Order ANSERIFORMES
Family Anatidae
    Cnemiornis [E]
    Euryanas [E]
    Hymenolaimus
    Pachyanas [E]

Order SPHENISCIFORMES
Family Spheniscidae
    Megadyptes

Order FALCONIFORMES
Family Accipitridae
    Harpagornis [E]

Order GRUIFORMES
Family Aptornithidae
    Aptornis [E]
Family Rallidae
    Capellirallus [E]
    Diaphorapteryx [E]

Order CHARADRIIFORMES
Family Scolopacidae
    Coenocorypha[1]
Family Charadriidae
    Anarhynchus

Order COLUMBIFORMES
Family Columbidae
    Hemiphaga[2]

Order PSITTACIFORMES
Family Psittacidae
    Strigops
    Nestor[2]

Order STRIGIFORMES
Family Strigidae
    Sceloglaux [E]

Order PASSERIFORMES
Family Acanthisittidae
    Acanthisitta
    Xenicus
    Traversia [E]
    Pachyplichas [E]
    Dendroscansor [E]
Family Turnagridae
    Turnagra [E]
Family Meliphagidae
    Notiomystis
    Anthornis
    Prosthemadera
Family Pachycephalidae
    Mohoua
Family Callaeidae
    Callaeas
    Philesturnus
    Heteralocha [E]
Family Corvidae
    Palaeocorax [E]
Family Sylviidae
    Bowdleria

[1] Bones of a *Coenocorypha* snipe have been found on Norfolk Island [HANZAB 3: 65].

[2] Also once found on Norfolk Island.

Table Two

The 120 Species of Birds
Endemic to the New Zealand Region

The 48 extinct species are marked [E]. Those living species restricted, or currently restricted, to outlying islands are marked [I]. The table shows the classification of the birds into orders and families. Species are excluded from this book that were extinct before New Zealand was first settled by humans.

Order STRUTHIONIFORMES
Family Emeidae
1. Little Bush Moa *Anomalopteryx didiformis* [E]
2. Upland Moa *Megalapteryx didinus* [E]
3. Heavy-footed Moa *Pachyornis elephantopus* [E]
4. Crested Moa *P. australis* [E]
5. Mappin's Moa *P. mappini* [E]
6. Eastern Moa *Emeus crassus* [E]
7. Stout-legged Moa *Euryapteryx geranoides* [E]
8. Coastal Moa *Eu. curtus* [E]

Family Dinornithidae
9. Slender Bush Moa *Dinornis struthoides* [E]
10. Large Bush Moa *D. novaezealandiae* [E]
11. Giant Moa *D. giganteus* [E]

Family Apterygidae
12. Brown Kiwi *Apteryx australis*
13. Little Spotted Kiwi *A. owenii*
14. Great Spotted Kiwi *A. haastii*

Order GALLIFORMES
Family Phasianidae
15. New Zealand Quail *Coturnix novaezelandiae* [E]

Order ANSERIFORMES
Family Anatidae
16. de Lautour's Duck *Biziura delautouri* [E]
17. New Zealand Swan *Cygnus sumnerensis* [E]
18. North Island Goose *Cnemiornis gracilis* [E]
19. South Island Goose *Cn. calcitrans* [E]
20. Finsch's Duck *Euryanas finschi* [E]
21. Paradise Shelduck *Tadorna variegata*
22. Blue Duck *Hymenolaimus malacorhynchos*
23. Brown Teal *Anas chlorotis*
24. Auckland Island Teal *A. aucklandica* [I]
25. Campbell Island Teal *A. nesiotis* [I]

Appendices

26. Chatham Island Duck *Pachyanas chathamica* [E] [I]
27. Scarlett's Duck *Malacorhynchus scarletti* [E]
28. New Zealand Scaup *Aythya novaeseelandiae*
29. Auckland Island Merganser *Mergus australis* [E]

Order PODICIPEDIFORMES
Family Podicipedidae
30. New Zealand Dabchick *Poliocephalus rufopectus*

Order SPHENISCIFORMES
Family Spheniscidae
31. Yellow-eyed Penguin *Megadyptes antipodes*
32. Fiordland Crested Penguin *Eudyptes pachyrhynchus*
33. Snares Crested Penguin *Eu. robustus* [I]
34. Erect-crested Penguin *Eu. sclateri* [I]

Order PROCELLARIIFORMES
Family Procellariidae
35. Buller's Shearwater *Puffinus bulleri*
36. Fluttering Shearwater *P. gavia*
37. Hutton's Shearwater *P. huttoni*
38. Scarlett's Shearwater *P. spelaeus* [E]
39. Black Petrel *Procellaria parkinsoni*
40. Westland Petrel *P. westlandica*
41. Pycroft's Petrel *Pterodroma pycrofti*
42. Cook's Petrel *Pt. cookii*
43. Mottled Petrel *Pt. inexpectata*
44. Chatham Petrel *Pt. axillaris* [I]
45. Magenta Petrel *Pt. magentae* [I]

Family Diomedeidae
46. Royal Albatross *Diomedea epomophora*
47. Buller's Mollymawk *Thalassarche bulleri*

Order PELECANIFORMES
Family Phalacrocoracidae
48. King Shag *Leucocarbo carunculatus*
49. Stewart Island Shag *L. chalconotus*
50. Chatham Island Shag *L. onslowi* [I]
51. Bounty Island Shag *L. ranfurlyi* [I]
52. Auckland Island Shag *L. colensoi* [I]
53. Campbell Island Shag *L. campbelli* [I]
54. Spotted Shag *Stictocarbo punctatus*
55. Pitt Island Shag *S. featherstoni* [I]

Family Pelecanidae
56. New Zealand Pelican *Pelecanus novaezealandiae* [E]

Order CICONIIFORMES
Family Ardeidae
57. New Zealand Little Bittern *Ixobrychus novaezelandiae* [E]

Order FALCONIFORMES
Family Accipitridae
58. Eyles' Harrier *Circus eylesi* [E]
59. Chatham Island Sea-eagle *Haliaeetus australis* [E] [I]
60. New Zealand Eagle *Harpagornis moorei* [E]

Family Falconidae
61. New Zealand Falcon *Falco novaeseelandiae*

Order GRUIFORMES
Family Aptornithidae
62. North Island Adzebill *Aptornis otidiformis* [E]
63. South Island Adzebill *A. defossor* [E]

Family Rallidae
64. Dieffenbach's Rail *Gallirallus dieffenbachii* [E] [I]
65. Chatham Island Rail *G. modestus* [E] [I]
66. Weka *G. australis*
67. Snipe-rail *Capellirallus karamu* [E]
68. Giant Chatham Island Rail *Diaphorapteryx hawkinsi* [E] [I]
69. North Island Takahe *Porphyrio mantelli* [E]
70. South Island Takahe *P. hochstetteri*
71. Hodgen's Rail *Gallinula hodgeni* [E]
72. New Zealand Coot *Fulica prisca* [E]
73. Chatham Island Coot *F. chathamensis* [E] [I]

Order CHARADRIIFORMES
Family Scolopacidae
74. New Zealand Snipe *Coenocorypha aucklandica* [I]
75. Chatham Island Snipe *C. pusilla* [I]
76. Giant Chatham Island Snipe *C. chathamica* [E] [I]

Family Haematopodidae
77. Variable Oystercatcher *Haematopus unicolor*
78. Chatham Island Oystercatcher *H. chathamensis* [I]

Family Recurvirostridae
79. Black Stilt *Himantopus novaezelandiae*

Family Charadriidae
80. New Zealand Dotterel *Charadrius obscurus*
81. Banded Dotterel *Ch. bicinctus*
82. Shore Plover *Thinornis novaeseelandiae* [I]
83. Wrybill *Anarhynchus frontalis*

Family Laridae
84. Black-billed Gull *Larus bulleri*
85. Black-fronted Tern *Sterna albostriata*

Order COLUMBIFORMES
Family Columbidae
86. New Zealand Pigeon *Hemiphaga novaeseelandiae*
87. Chatham Island Pigeon *H. chathamensis* [I]

Order PSITTACIFORMES
Family Psittacidae
88. Kakapo *Strigops habroptilus*
89. Kaka *Nestor meridionalis*
90. Kea *N. notabilis*
91. Yellow-crowned Parakeet *Cyanoramphus auriceps*
92. Antipodes Island Parakeet *C. unicolor* [I]

Order CUCULIFORMES
Family Cuculidae
93. Long-tailed Cuckoo *Eudynamys taitensis*

Order STRIGIFORMES
Family Strigidae
94. Laughing Owl *Sceloglaux albifacies* [E]

Order CAPRIMULGIFORMES
Family Aegothelidae
95. New Zealand Owlet-nightjar *Aegotheles novaezealandiae* [E]

Order PASSERIFORMES
Family Acanthisittidae
96. Rifleman *Acanthisitta chloris*
97. Bush Wren *Xenicus longipes* [E]
98. Rock Wren *X. gilviventris*
99. Stephens Island Wren *Traversia lyalli* [E]
100. Grant-Mackie's Wren *Pachyplichas jagmi* [E]
101. Yaldwyn's Wren *P. yaldwyni* [E]
102. Long-billed Wren *Dendroscansor decurvirostris* [E]

Family Turnagridae
103. Piopio *Turnagra capensis* [E]

Family Pardalotidae
104. Grey Warbler *Gerygone igata*
105. Chatham Island Warbler *G. albofrontata* [I]

Family Meliphagidae
106. Stitchbird *Notiomystis cincta*
107. Bellbird *Anthornis melanura*
108. Tui *Prosthemadera novaeseelandiae*

Family Petroicidae
109. New Zealand Tomtit *Petroica macrocephala*
110. New Zealand Robin *P. australis*
111. Black Robin *P. traversi* [I]

Family Pachycephalidae
112. Whitehead *Mohoua albicilla*
113. Yellowhead *M. ochrocephala*
114. Brown Creeper *M. novaeseelandiae*

Family Callaeidae
115. Kokako *Callaeas cinerea*
116. Saddleback *Philesturnus carunculatus*
117. Huia *Heteralocha acutirostris* [E]

Family Corvidae
118. New Zealand Crow *Palaeocorax moriorum* [E]

Family Sylviidae
119. Fernbird *Bowdleria punctata*
120. Chatham Island Fernbird *B. rufescens* [E] [I]

Table Three
Species of New Zealand Birds
Endemic to Certain Islands

Based on total range for land birds, and breeding range for others, including prehistoric distributions not just current distributions.

North Island
Mappin's Moa
Coastal Moa
North Island Goose
North Island Adzebill
Snipe-rail
North Island Takahe
Grant-Mackie's Wren
Stitchbird
Whitehead
Huia

South Island
Upland Moa
Heavy-footed Moa
Crested Moa
Eastern Moa
Great Spotted Kiwi
South Island Goose
Hutton's Shearwater
Scarlett's Shearwater
Westland Petrel
Stewart Island Shag
South Island Adzebill
South Island Takahe
Wrybill
Black-fronted Tern
Yaldwyn's Wren
Long-billed Wren
Yellowhead
Brown Creeper

Chatham Islands
Chatham Island Duck
Chatham Petrel
Magenta Petrel
Chatham Island Shag
Pitt Island Shag
Chatham Island Sea-eagle
Dieffenbach's Rail
Chatham Island Rail
Giant Chatham Island Rail
Chatham Island Coot
Chatham Island Snipe
Giant Chatham Island Snipe
Chatham Island Oystercatcher
Chatham Island Pigeon
Chatham Island Warbler
Black Robin
Chatham Island Fernbird

Subantarctic Islands
Auckland Island Teal
Campbell Island Teal
Snares Crested Penguin
Erect-crested Penguin
Bounty Island Shag
Auckland Island Shag
Campbell Island Shag
Antipodes Island Parakeet

Table Four: The 34 Endemic Subspecies of New Zealand Birds (belonging to species not endemic)

Swans, Geese and Ducks (Family Anatidae)
1. New Zealand Shoveler (Kuruwhengi) *Anas rhynchotis variegata* (Gould, 1856)

Penguins (Family Spheniscidae)
2. Blue Penguin (Korora) *Eudyptula minor minor* (Forster, 1781) [number of subspecies endemic to New Zealand unresolved, but at least one]

Shearwaters, Fulmars, Prions and Petrels (Family Procellariidae)
3. North Island Little Shearwater *Puffinus assimilis haurakiensis* Fleming and Serventy, 1943
4. Kermadec Little Shearwater *P. assimilis kermadecensis* Murphy, 1927
5. Snares Cape Pigeon *Daption capense australe* Mathews, 1913
6. Chatham Fulmar Prion *Pachyptila crassirostris pyramidalis* Fleming, 1939
7. Grey-faced Petrel (Oi) *Pterodroma macroptera gouldi* (Hutton, 1869)

Albatrosses and Mollymawks (Family Diomedeidae)
8. Antipodean Wandering Albatross *Diomedea exulans antipodensis* Robertson and Warham, 1992
9. Gibson's Wandering Albatross *D. exulans gibsoni* Robertson and Warham, 1992
10. New Zealand Black-browed Mollymawk *Thalassarche melanophrys impavida* Mathews, 1912
11. New Zealand White-capped Mollymawk *Th. cauta steadi* Falla, 1933
12. Chatham Island Mollymawk *Th. cauta eremita* Murphy, 1930

Storm Petrels (Family Hydrobatidae)
13. New Zealand White-faced Storm Petrel (Takahikare-moana) *Pelagodroma marina maoriana* Mathews, 1912

Cormorants and Shags (Family Phalacrocoracidae)
14. Little Shag (Kawaupaka) *Phalacrocorax melanoleucos brevirostris* Gould, 1837
15. Pied Shag (Karuhiruhi) *Phalacrocorax varius varius* (Gmelin, 1789)

Rails, Gallinules and Coots (Family Rallidae)
16. Banded Rail (Moho-pereru) *Gallirallus philippensis assimilis* (G.R. Gray, 1843)
17. Auckland Island Rail *Rallus pectoralis muelleri* Rothschild, 1893
18. Marsh Crake (Koitareke) *Porzana pusilla affinis* (J.E. Gray, 1845)

Oystercatchers (Family Haematopodidae)
19. South Island Pied Oystercatcher (Torea) *Haematopus ostralegus finschi* Martens, 1897

Gulls and Terns (Family Laridae)
20. Red-billed Gull (Tarapunga) *Larus novaehollandiae scopulinus* J.R. Forster, 1844
21. New Zealand Fairy Tern *Sterna nereis davisae* (Mathews and Iredale, 1913)

Parrots and Lorikeets (Family Psittacidae)
22. Red-crowned Parakeet (Kakariki) *Cyanoramphus novaezelandiae novaezelandiae* (Sparrman, 1787)
23. Kermadec Parakeet *C. novaezelandiae cyanurus* Salvadori, 1891
24. Chatham Island Red-crowned Parakeet *C. novaezelandiae chathamensis* Oliver, 1930
25. Reischek's Parakeet *C. novaezelandiae hochstetteri* (Reischek, 1889)

Typical Owls (Family Strigidae)
26. Morepork (Ruru) *Ninox novaeseelandiae novaeseelandiae* (Gmelin, 1788)

Forest Kingfishers (Family Halcyonidae)
27. New Zealand Kingfisher (Kotare) *Todiramphus sanctus vagans* (Lesson, 1830)

Fantails and Allies (Family Dicruridae)
28. North Island Fantail (Piwakawaka) *Rhipidura fuliginosa placabilis* Bangs, 1921
29. South Island Fantail (Piwakawaka) *Rh. fuliginosa fuliginosa* (Sparrman, 1787)
30. Chatham Island Fantail *Rh. fuliginosa penita* Bangs, 1911

Wagtails and Pipits (Family Motacillidae)
31. New Zealand Pipit (Pihoihoi) *Anthus novaeseelandiae novaeseelandiae* (Gmelin, 1789)
32. Chatham Island Pipit *A. novaeseelandiae chathamensis* Lorenz-Liburnau, 1902
33. Auckland Island Pipit *A. novaeseelandiae aucklandicus* G.R. Gray, 1862
34. Antipodes Island Pipit *A. novaeseelandiae steindachneri* Reischek, 1889

Index

This index contains reference to the individual entries for birds in this book. Italicised numbers indicate illustrations.

Antipodes Island Parakeet   105, *105*
Auckland Island Merganser   44
Auckland Island Shag   66
Auckland Island Teal   42, *43*
Australasian Bittern   154, *155*
Australasian Gannet   152, *152*
Australasian Harrier   177, *177*
Australasian Shoveler   *144*, 145
Banded Dotterel   89, *89, 90*
Banded Rail   158, *158*
Bar-tailed Godwit   160, 161, *161*
Bellbird   122, *122, 123*
Black Petrel   56, *57*
Black Robin   129, *129*
Black Shag   153, *153*
Black Stilt   85, *85, 86*
Black-backed Gull   166, *167*
Black-billed Gull   93, 94, *94*
Black-browed Mollymawk   151
Black-fronted Tern   95, *95*
Black-winged Petrel   150
Blue Duck   40, *40, 41*
Blue Penguin   147, *147*
Bounty Island Shag   66
Broad-billed Prion   149
Brown Creeper   132, *132*
Brown Kiwi   30, 31, *31*
Brown Teal   42, *42*
Buller's Mollymawk   62, *62*
Buller's Shearwater   53, 54, *54*
Bush Wren   112, *113*
Campbell Island Shag   66
Campbell Island Teal   43
Cape Pigeon   150, *150*
Caspian Tern   166, *167*
Chatham Island Coot   80
Chatham Island Duck   43
Chatham Island Fernbird   141, *141*
Chatham Island Oystercatcher   84

Chatham Island Pigeon   98
Chatham Island Rail   75, *76*
Chatham Island Sea-eagle   71
Chatham Island Shag   66
Chatham Island Snipe   81, *81*
Chatham Island Warbler   120
Chatham Petrel   60
Coastal Moa   28, *28, 29*
Common Diving Petrel   150
Cook's Petrel   59, *59*
Crested Moa   27
Curlew Sandpiper   *162*
de Latour's Duck   37
Dieffenbach's Rail   75
Eastern Curlew   161
Eastern Moa   28, *28*
Erect-crested Penguin   51
Eurasian Coot   158, *159*
Eyles' Harrier   71
Fairy Prion   150
Fairy Tern   168
Fernbird   139, *139, 140, 141*
Finsch's Duck   38
Fiordland Crested Penguin   50, *50, 51*
Flesh-footed Shearwater   148, 149, *149*
Fluttering Shearwater   55, *55*
Giant Chatham Island Rail   78, *78*
Giant Chatham Island Snipe   81
Giant Moa   28, 29, *29*
Grant-Mackie's Wren   115
Great Crested Grebe   146, *146*
Great Spotted Kiwi   33, *33*
Grey Duck   *144*, 145
Grey Teal   115, *115*
Grey Warbler   118, 119, *119*, 170
Grey-faced Petrel   150, *150*
Heavy-footed Moa   27
Hodgen's Rail   80
Huia   137, *137*

Hutton's Shearwater   56
Kaka   102, *102*
Kakapo   100, *100, 101*
Kea   103, *103, 104*
King Shag   64, *64*
Kokako   133, *134, 134*
Large Bush Moa   29
Laughing Owl   108, *108*
Lesser Knot   161, *162*
Little Bush Moa   27
Little Shag   153, *153*
Little Shearwater   149, *149*
Little Spotted Kiwi   32, *32*
Long-billed Wren   115
Long-tailed Cuckoo   106, *107*
Magenta Petrel   60
Mappin's Moa   27
Marsh Crake   158
Morepork   171, *171*
Mottled Petrel   59
New Zealand Coot   80
New Zealand Crow   138, *138*
New Zealand Dabchick   46, *47, 47*
New Zealand Dotterel   87, *87, 88*
New Zealand Eagle   71, *71*
New Zealand Falcon   72, 73, *73*
New Zealand (Grey) Fantail   173, *173*
New Zealand Kingfisher   172, *172*
New Zealand Little Bittern   69
New Zealand Owlet-nightjar   109
New Zealand Pelican   68
New Zealand Pigeon   96, 97, *97*, 98
New Zealand Pipit   174, *174*
New Zealand Quail   35, *35*
New Zealand Robin   128, *128*
New Zealand Scaup   44, *44, 45*
New Zealand Snipe   82
New Zealand Swan   37
New Zealand Tomtit   126, *126, 127*

North Island Adzebill   75
North Island Goose   37
North Island Takahe   78
Northern Giant Petrel   150, *150*
Pacific Golden Plover   165, *165*
Paradise Shelduck   38, *38, 39*
Pied Shag   153
Pied Stilt   164, *164*
Piopio   117, *117*
Pitt Island Shag   68
Pukeko   158, *159*
Pycroft's Petrel   58, *58*
Red-billed Gull   166, *167*
Red-crowned Parakeet   169, *169*
Red-necked Stint   161
Reef Heron   154, *154*
Rifleman   111, *111, 112*
Rock Wren   113, *113, 114*
Royal Albatross   60, 61, *61*
Royal Spoonbill   156, *156*
Saddleback   135, *135, 136*

Scarlett's Duck   43
Scarlett's Shearwater   56
Shining Cuckoo   170, *170*
Shore Plover   91, *91*
Silvereye   176, *176*
Slender Bush Moa   29
Snares Crested Penguin   51
Snipe-rail   78
Sooty Shearwater   *148*, 149
South Island Adzebill   75, *75*
South Island Goose   37, *37*
South Island Pied Oystercatcher   163, *163*
South Island Takahe   78, *78, 79*
Spotless Crake   158, *159*
Spotted Shag   67, *67, 68*
Spur-winged Plover   165, *165*
Stephens Island Wren   114
Stewart Island Shag   64, 65
Stitchbird   120, *120, 121*
Stout-legged Moa   28
Tui   124, *124, 125*

Turnstone   161, *162*
Upland Moa   27
Variable Oystercatcher   83, 84, *84*
Wandering Albatross   151
Wandering Tattler   *162*
Weka   76, *76, 77*
Welcome Swallow   175, *175*
Westland Petrel   56, 57, *57*
White Heron   154, *154*
White-capped (Shy) Mollymawk   151, *151*
White-faced Heron   154, *154*
White-faced Storm Petrel   151, *151*
White-fronted Tern   166, *166*, 168, *168*
Whitehead   130, 131, *131*
Wrybill   91, *91*, 92
Yaldwyn's Wren   115
Yellow-crowned Parakeet   104, *104*
Yellow-eyed Penguin   48, 49, *49*
Yellowhead   131, *131*

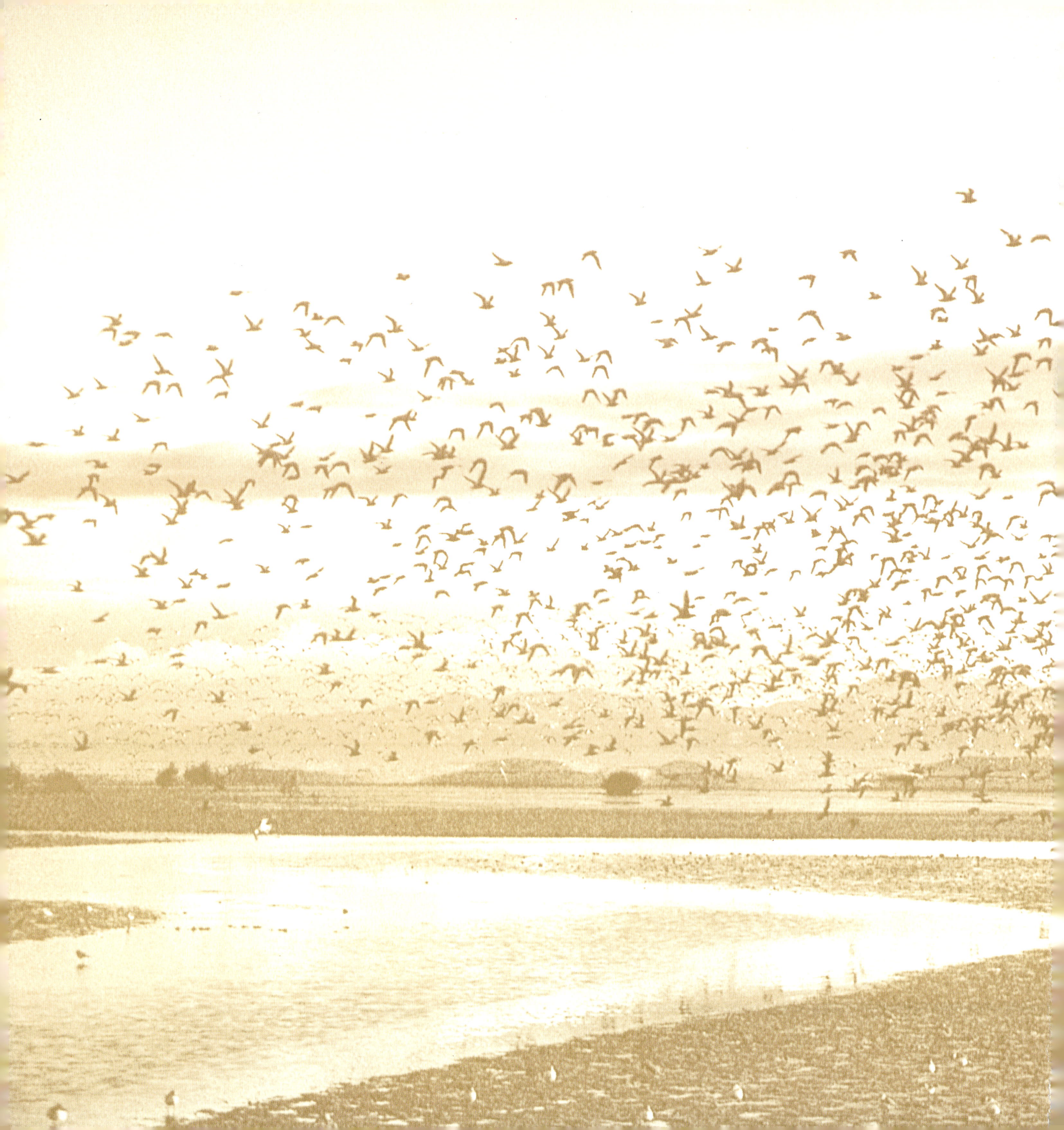